In Praise

A life well lived, and a ... g, a longtime friend and mentor, asked me to review *Rowing Against the Waves*, and found myself caught up in a tale of a typical American life spent making the world a better place.

Linda Gallagher
Editor, retired
West Shore Publications

What an amazing legacy Reg has left for future generations, for not only his family, but all of us. His story of a young boy growing up in rural Northern Michigan during the great depression is eye opening. It captures a picture of daily life that has long since passed and is being forgotten, but is important for all of us to understand, that ultimately led to the creation of the greatest generation. Being from Manton, it was captivating to learn the history of the town and surrounding area. Reg's 1946 basketball team is still the only MHSAA team championship in Manton's history and the detailed account of that season and how that team came to be is amazing. I hope this book inspires others to pass along information of where they come from on to future generations. As each generation passes away, the history of that individual family and how they came to be the people they are often passes with them. We need more people like Reg to document their story and pass it along for future generations. Thank you, Reg, for this fascinating look at life that is quickly being forgotten in our fast-paced 21st century world.

Leonard G. Morrow, Jr.
Superintendent of Schools - Manton, MI

"I am filled with gratitude for the gift of another day" — Reggie Sprik. Reggie's autobiography is a gift to the reader. In this charming reminiscence Reggie treats the reader to a trip down memory lane. While the details are his own, the memories belong to all of us. Reggie has captured the essence of midwestern life in the twentieth century. His family history, as progeny of Dutch immigrants arriving to Michigan in 1890, is a shining example of America and Americana. Getting to know Reggie through his detailed, insightful writing, readers "of a certain age" will recognize their parents' old stories, their own lived experiences, and the future that they now leave to their children and grandchildren. The reader learns of Reggie's early life as a poor (and hard-headed) farm boy who grows into a gifted high school and college athlete. Reggie shares his midlife experiences from military service through raising his own family in the 1960s. Evidence of his determination to continue to contribute to his community in his golden years is evident from his involvement as a local musician and ongoing service to local sports and educational endeavors. Reggie's life is almost a cliché. But cliché in the best sense — it gives today's reader reassurance; things to think about and perhaps things to aspire to in this age where the value of a good fishing story has given way to the latest viral TikTok video. This book belongs on the shelf of every collector of grassroots American history, and every library in lower Michigan. And it certainly belongs in the hands of every reader that enjoys the warm feeling of nostalgia.

Mary Richards
Elementary Teacher, Retired - Alba, MI

Reggie is raised in object poverty by a loving extended family during The Great Depression followed by World War II. His story is a narrative that flows along as he discovers that he is a fine athlete. He moves his team to become Michigan basketball champions, against great odds.

Reggie again amazed himself and his family beyond belief when he walks on Western Michigan College practice football field, without ever having played highschool football, and makes the team. Soon, he becomes a star player.

Desire!

His story goes on to show how Reggie and his wife, Marilyn, struggle to raise their family in northern Michigan with the same loving attitude that his family gave him.

In the end, it seems that Reggie has not given up his principals of working hard and fair play, but he may have improved his approach.

The story narrative flows along from one topic to the next much as Reggie's life may have moved.

It was so interesting to me that I completed it in one read, and I am still thinking about it.

> "We lived and learned, life threw curves,
> There was joy and there was hurt,
> Remember when?"
> — Alan Jackson

John Fichtner
Elementary and Middle School Principal, Retired - Mancelona, MI

.

ROWING AGAINST
THE WAVES

Published by Mission Point Press
2554 Chandler Rd.
Traverse City, MI 49696
(231) 421-9513
www.MissionPointPress.com

ISBN 9781958363409
Library of Congress Control Number 2022917223

Printed in the United States of America

ROWING AGAINST
THE WAVES

Overcoming Adversities,
Leading to a Life Well Lived

REG SPRIK

MISSION POINT PRESS

Dedication

To my beautiful wife, Marilyn, who lives on in my heart,

and to our children Dave, Bob, Jan and Nancy.

Contents

- Chapter One -
Early Days—Ancestors

The gooey mud tugged at my mini feet as I laboriously trudged toward our temporary residence, the parsonage of the Arlene Christian Reformed Church. It was tough going, but I knew I had to make it there. I was on my own. I was, also, three years old, and it was my first memory of the life of this writer on planet Earth.

Neither of my parents, Ed or Margaret Aten Sprik, was a church pastor, and our family did not occupy this parsonage by choice. The Wall Street Crash of 1929 set in motion an economic downturn which displaced us from our rented home in Detroit. Automobile manufacturers began laying off workers, and my dad was employed just two days a week.

There was no state or federal unemployment agency at that time. Men, who were usually the sole income producers for their families and who were living in the ubiquitous apartment complexes, were unable to pay the rent and buy groceries for their families. The soup lines were long, and my dad witnessed desperate men climbing up on soapboxes and park benches in Cadillac Square in downtown Detroit calling, angrily, for "revolution!"

In the meantime, my mother's room and board business was falling apart, as the Scottish guests were losing their jobs and were forced to relocate.

The small northern Lower Michigan community of Arlene, where my parents spent early years, soon learned of our plight. The local Arlene church parsonage was temporarily unoccupied, and my parents were invited to move in for the time being. We lived there three months.

When it comes to the life of this writer, however, it did not all begin as a struggling three-year-old in a muddy Arlene field. Each person brings into the world vestiges of those who have traveled the earthly road of his or her heritage. It might be in appearance, voice, talents, as well as other characteristics. But, the building blocks of who we are as a person have been laid over considerable time by ancestors, some of whom we know little about. So, as we travel back in time, let's look at some of those people who have something to do with the author of this life story.

Grandpa Jacob Aten came to the United States with Grandma Marchien Aten in 1890. They came from a small community known as Odoorn in the province of Groningen in the northern part of the Netherlands. They were in their late thirties when they arrived with their family at Ellis Island, and neither of them could speak a word of English.

Grandpa and Grandma Aten had left behind a life in the bottom tier of a grossly unfair caste system, in which they could never own property or get an education. Those privileges were reserved for those born into a higher social classification.

A few years after locating in the Arlene area, Grandpa and Grandma Aten had by then saved a little money and were able to buy what amounted to forty acres of stump-covered, unproductive blow sand. They were immensely proud of their land purchase. The water table near their house was not suitable for a water well, so they carried water from a spring below a hill for household and livestock needs.

Grandpa Aten cleared their land of pine stumps to allow for growing a few crops and a large garden. He also worked as a carpenter and sold firewood. The family foraged for much of its food and kept a large number of chickens for both eggs and meat.

Grandma Aten was admired for her warm, loving nature. She had learned the tailoring trade as a young person in the Netherlands and was a master craftsperson with a sewing machine.

As Grandpa and Grandma Aten neared retirement years, Grandpa Aten built a four- room house with a small barn and a chicken coop very near the Arlene church and country store. There, they lived out their retirement years. After being widowed, however, Grandpa Aten temporarily lived elsewhere.

There were eight children in the Jacob and Marchien Aten family. Hattie, Frederica (later known as "Rica"), Marchien (my mother, whose name became "Margaret"), and Henry were all born in the Netherlands. The other four children were born in the United States. They were in order: Ralph, Jay, Gertrude, and Herman.

Jacob and Marchien (Meijer) Aten Family - back row l to r: Margaret, Ralph, Jay, Fredrica, Henry, Hattie. Front row l to r: Marchien, Herm, Gertrude, Jacob.

Grandpa Harm Sprik was born in the United States and Grandma Jane Brink Sprik was born in the Netherlands, but all of their ancestors were from the Netherlands. Harm was a large man, estimated to be more than six feet tall and well over two hundred pounds. He grew up in an abusive home setting, and as often happens in such cases, he carried that cruel legacy into the parenting of his sons.

Harm and Jane (Brink) Sprik Family - back row l to r: Ed, Bert, John.
Front row l to r: Harm, Lou, Jane, Jennie.

He grew up on a farm in the Holland/Zeeland area of western Michigan, and there had been episodes of violence in his younger days. He paid a price for his early behavior, however, as in at least one case, a person vowed revenge. As a result, he would not enter his barn alone at night, and if there was a knock on the door at night, he carried a stove poker in his hand in response.

Early Days–Ancestors

On the other hand, he could be exceedingly hospitable, often inviting neighbors, passing by with horses and wagons, to come into the house for a cup of coffee.

In spite of the fact that he was very rough and demanding with his sons and farm employees, he was very good to Grandma Jane. He hired a full-time, live-in maid to help her with cooking and household chores, and each summer he paid for her three-week vacation to the Holland area, so she could visit family and friends.

Very little is known about the background of Grandma Jane Sprik. She was known to be a very kind, loving individual, held in very high regard by everyone who knew her.

There were five living children in the Harm and Jane Sprik family: Evert ("Ed," my dad), John, Bert, Lou, and Jennie. One daughter didn't survive and is buried in the Norwood, Michigan Cemetery.

My mother, Marchien Aten, was born in the small community of Odoorn, located in the northern part of the Netherlands. At the age of two, she, her parents, two sisters, and one brother immigrated to the United States.

The family originally lived in Grand Rapids, Michigan, but soon settled in the predominantly Dutch community called Arlene, where they lived with a host family until my Grandpa Jacob Aten could build a temporary residence.

My mother's name was translated to "Margaret" from the original "Marchien." At age five, my mother began attending the nearby Dingman School. Her teacher at the Dingman school was a young lady named Emma. My mother greatly admired Emma. But, there was a problem. Due to the severe winters in the Arlene area, the Dingman school was forced to close during winter months. My mother, who loved going to school, soon learned of an alternative.

The Doyle school remained open through the winter, and when

my mother could no longer attend the Dingman school, she walked the extra distance through snow and ice to attend the Doyle school. She spoke highly of the male teacher at Doyle school, who, according to my mother, was a strict disciplinarian.

Standards were very high in the one-room country schools at that time. Students were held back from promotion to the next grade until certain standards were met. In order to graduate from eighth grade and possibly enter high school, a student needed to pass a state board examination. Because of a lack of transportation, many students did not go on to high school.

Upon graduating from eighth grade, my mother wanted to go on to high school. She greatly enjoyed the learning environment of a schoolroom, and she wanted to continue on to become a nurse.

Their family home was five miles from the nearest town, however, and the high school was just too far away to walk alone in the wintertime. Furthermore, she couldn't deal with homesickness, which would have been a factor if she lived in town and worked for her room and board. Consequently, she earned money by working as a maid for families that lived near her home. She often spoke of her experiences working for the White family. The Whites were homesteaders and were among the first settlers in the area. Mr. Jim White was a Civil War veteran. My mother thought highly of the White family.

During summers, she and two of her cousins picked huckleberries and blackberries, then sold them to wives of lumber barons in the town of Jennings. Black bears are known to be fond of ripe berries, and my mother and her cousins were very much aware of that fact. They discussed methods of saving themselves if just such a scenario came about.

They developed a plan. If they came head-on with a bear in the berry patch, one of them would quickly remove her apron, tie it around the bear's neck, and choke the bear to death. Lo and behold, the fruits of their imaginations actually turned into reality. A black bear suddenly arose on hind legs directly in front of them. Sometimes, the best of plans simply do not work out. Instead of tying apron strings, they tried to break speed records fleeing in the opposite direction. Over time, the berry picking continued, as the money earned was needed to cover the cost of new clothes. The berry patch bear encounter was not the last of Margaret Aten's hair-raising outdoor experiences, however.

It so happened that the Aten family home was located in a remote area, about two miles from the local church, the center of most Aten family activities. Many young men and women of the community attended Bible studies at that location, most of which took place in the evening. At the conclusion of these events, Margaret Aten was usually invited to ride home in a horse and buggy with one of the boys in the group. But, on one such evening, an invitation did not come about and my mother was compelled to walk the two miles home.

The night was totally dark, with no sign of moonlight to light the way. My mother was barely able to follow the wagon trail leading back to her home. Walking completely alone through swamps and woodland, she suddenly heard the unmistakable scream and growl of a nearby mountain lion.

Veteran campers and hunters will nearly always proclaim that there is no sound in the outback as terrifying as the piercing scream and growl of a mountain lion. Nearly petrified with fear, my mother remembered being warned not to run from a predator. Step-by-step, Margaret walked along, fearing with each step that certain death lurked with each forward movement. Finally, she stepped through the door to her house and quickly closed the door behind her. She told this story many times. Maybe it was her way of reflecting on the struggles of her early life.

My parents were what used to be called "full-blooded Dutch." That's Netherlands Dutch, not Pennsylvania Dutch, who are of German descent. My dad, whose grandfather and grandmother were born and raised in the Netherlands, was brought into the world in Antrim County, Michigan, near the little town of Norwood in September 1888. His formal education was what might be called "seasonal," and it's doubtful that he ever completed eighth grade. My dad's father was known to knock on the school door during spring planting and fall harvest time. "I need Ed to work today," he would tell the teacher. That happened frequently, my mother told me, so it is likely my dad was actually in school mostly during winter months only. But the end result was surprising.

Although my father's spelling was not the best, his written and spoken English were clear and concise. And, although he never wasted words, he was an excellent communicator. But that's not the best part.

My father was an absolute math whiz. Since I was a rather poor arithmetic student, I was constantly amazed at the ease with which he dealt with our entire decimal system, mostly in his head, no less, without putting anything on paper. My older brothers, with high school diplomas and high math classes in their credentials, could not come close to competing with my dad when it came to working with numbers. Born before his time in that regard, he had an aptitude for engineering, computer programming, or, because he was very popular with youth groups in church, he could very well have become a high school or college math teacher. His shortcomings were far outweighed by his many strong qualities.

In his earlier years, he worked on the family farm during summers and in lumber camps during the cold months. In those days, trees were felled with axes, and he was one of the best at bringing down the large white pine trees that were targeted by lumber barons of the day. Although my father was not a powerfully built man, he knew how to make any tool, and particularly a double-bitted ax, work to his advantage. Because he had become an expert at working with horses,

Ed Sprik atop logs as a teamster in a logging camp.

Ed Sprik (on right) with friend using cant hook in a northern Michigan logging camp.

he soon became a teamster in the logging camps. He would drive a team, pulling a sleigh piled high with logs, to meet the narrow gauge railway train that would then haul the logs to the sawmill. It was dangerous work.

That was especially true when the driver needed to take the horses down a slippery slope. Unless the entire situation was carefully managed, it would be possible for the sleigh load of logs to overrun the horses. It doesn't require much imagination to visualize the results of that kind of scenario. He continued to live at home, working the fields in summer and logging camps in winter until, when in his early twenties, an event took place that forever changed the direction of his life.

It so happened that relatives lived near Chicago, where they owned and operated a produce farm. Throughout summers they brought vegetables and fruits into Chicago by horse and wagon and sold the produce at various markets within the city. Since my dad enjoyed meeting people and was an expert teamster, he was perfectly suited to that type of work. Still living at home, however, my dad had to help with farm work.

Grandpa Harm, who had grown up in a rough and tough environment, had a hair-trigger temper. Something my father either did, or did not do, lit my grandfather's fuse. While my dad was tending one of the horses in a stall, Grandpa Harm physically charged him. My dad was literally being choked by my grandfather's forearm, which Grandpa Harm used to pin my dad against the side of the horse stall. Somehow, my dad broke free. He immediately left to live with, and work for, his Chicago relatives. It was his first experience in marketing, and it sparked a lifetime interest in the business field.

Ed Sprik (directly behind horses) in Chicago.

Early Days–Ancestors

Ed and Margaret (Aten) Sprik in a serious mode.

My mother's work as a household maid took her to various locations including Petoskey and Charlevoix. Eventually, she was hired to work in the Harm and Jane Sprik home. At that point, Ed and Margaret came to know each other well and a romantic relationship developed. But, Ed's unexpected departure for Chicago disrupted their connection. My dad wanted to stay in Chicago, but my mother didn't want to live there. Not wanting to break up their romance, Ed moved back to Arlene. They were each twenty-four years of age.

Ed Sprik and Margaret Aten were married on June 12, 1913. Immediately after their wedding, Ed and Margaret left to live in McBain, Michigan, where they joined Ed's brother, John, and his wife, Bessie, in a cream station business. My oldest brother, Harold, was born in McBain in early summer 1914.

The cream station business did not work out, however, and while John and Bessie moved to Park Lake, Ed and Margaret moved to Manton, where they bought a general store. While owning and managing the Manton store, my dad made the mistake of letting out too much credit. Typically, business owners of that time kept notebooks, each with a customer's name. Customers were expected to "settle up" on payday. But, as one might expect, that didn't always happen. Unable or unwilling to "pay up" on payday, customers drifted over to the other two Manton general stores to buy weekly supplies. This resulted in my parents' inability to restock shelves. At that point, in order to save their business, my parents embarked on what turned out to be a disastrous borrowing plan.

Money was borrowed from parents, and uncles and aunts, but eventually, unable to restock shelves or pay back loans, the business collapsed. Ed and Margaret were forced to sell their store. Bankruptcy was not an option, as my dad considered bankruptcy dishonest and a form of thievery. He refused to lower his personal standards.

By that time, John Sprik, dad's younger brother, had moved his family to Detroit. My dad learned that factory work was plentiful there. The goal of my dad was to pay back the money he had borrowed. A factory job in Detroit offered that opportunity. Limited to an eighth-grade education, professional level work was not an option.

The twenties were roaring, and the Ed and Margaret Sprik family landed in the midst of it. American society was rapidly changing from the horse and buggy age to the days of the horseless carriage. Automobile factories were popping up throughout the Detroit general area. Brand names included Packard, LaSalle, Rio, Falcon/Knight, as well as Ford, etc. Most were poorly engineered—their products failed for various reasons shortly after being purchased and put into use, and the companies were soon out of business.

But, plenty of work was available and Ed Sprik spent part of his time as a buffer at the Fisher Body Plant. The job involved standing in front of a buffing wheel, by the hour, holding metal auto parts to a machine in order to make the parts bright and gleaming.

Having grown up in an outdoor environment on a farm and in lumber camps, my dad was a total misfit in the stifling surroundings of a manufacturing plant. He hated the work, and judging from the family's series of rental residences, he probably was fired from or quit numerous factory jobs. In one case, in particular, he was undoubtedly instantly terminated.

Labor unions were not yet well established in the auto industry and intimidation was the main means of motivating employees. It was a time in manufacturing when industry used a "straw boss" type of management. These individuals were men who worked on machines along with other production workers but filled in for foremen when called upon. Since they worked on machines along with other production workers, they were looked upon somewhat as traitors and were universally detested.

On one occasion, my dad needed a particular tool in order to make an adjustment on a machine on which he was working. He requested the device from his straw boss. The straw boss left, as if to secure the needed tool. When he returned, my dad held out his hand to receive the tool. Instead of placing the tool in my dad's hand, the straw boss spit in my dad's open hand.

Ed Sprik was one of the most nonviolent individuals one could imagine. Throughout his life, he had stoically endured one hardship after another. But, he had a breaking point. Without thinking, he raised his hand and rubbed the saliva over the face of the straw boss. Although he did not explain the outcome of this episode, this was another time he was likely fired on the spot.

While my dad labored in various factories, my mother also contributed to the family income by taking in roomers and boarders. Several young men from Scotland had immigrated to Detroit seeking factory work. Scotland offered little, if any, employment for young, single men at that time. With a background as a farm girl, my mother knew how to fill their bellies at little cost. She realized the importance of volume, so she provided large bowls of spaghetti, mashed potatoes, oatmeal, and other meals made from scratch. It's likely she also laundered their clothing. Since my parents rented at least two different houses plus an apartment, it's unknown the exact length of time my parents provided food and shelter for the young Scots.

Ed Sprik cradles brother Ray in his arm while entertaining Scottie in Manton while owning the General Store.

Then, there was the dog named "Scottie," no connection to the roomers and boarders. Scottie accompanied our family in the move from Manton to Detroit. He was deeply loved by the family, particularly my mother. Scottie was a collie, and as such, he guarded the property with serious dedication. Dogs of Scottie's breeding have a reputation of risking life and limb in order to protect the well-being and property of their master. This shepherding characteristic brought on considerable embarrassment and, in another era, the potential for legal action against my parents.

The era of horse transportation was coming to an end, and sporty automobiles were making their way onto the streets. It's well to remember that streets were much narrower then, so automobiles passed very near houses. A neighboring gentleman owned one of these elaborate cars, known as a touring car. Headlights were prominent, fenders were wide, and the canvas roof was retractable.

One day this neighbor came driving past my parent's rental home. An English bulldog rode on each front fender. Scottie happened to be loose in the front yard, and his natural shepherd instincts immediately came into play. Racing into the street, he jerked a bulldog off the nearest fender and began to administer an old-fashioned farm dog thrashing. Fortunately, my mother was nearby and was soon able to get the situation under control. Profuse apologies by my mother were enough to ease the situation, and the young man went on his way. My mother had a special loving connection to Scottie. But, Scottie was a farm dog, unsuited for city life, and ultimately, he had to be given away to an owner with a more appropriate environment.

The eighteenth amendment to the constitution, ratified on January 16, 1919, and referred to as "prohibition," had a profound effect on society in Detroit during that era. That amendment made it illegal to manufacture, sell, or transport intoxicating liquors within the United States and its territories.

The amendment was generally considered to be an infringement on individual rights. Beer and whiskey were manufactured and sold in basements, garages, and attics. They were called "speakeasies" because of their secrecy. They bloomed throughout cities everywhere. Much of the illegal alcohol came across the border from Canada, where brewing and drinking were legal.

Furthermore, it was a time of unprecedented prosperity. World War I, "the war to end all wars," had ended victoriously for the United States and its allies in 1918. Henry Ford had invented the Model T and subsequently the Model A, cars that sold for well under one thousand dollars, within the financial range of the average worker. It was the time of the "flapper," "Hey you kid," and dancing the Charleston into the night.

A surge in spending accompanied the general prosperity of the times. Stocks began to rise in value and people began to buy into the stock market. As stock prices escalated, it became apparent that one could borrow money from a bank to invest in stocks with nothing but the stocks themselves as security for the loans.

Eventually, as more and more bank capital became invested in stocks, bank officials became concerned about their enormous volume of precariously secured funds being lent to their customers, and the banks began calling in their loans. Consequently, stockholders were forced to sell their holdings in order to pay their loans. The law of supply and demand quickly took over and stock prices began to drop.

As shareholders began to see the value of their portfolios declining, panic began to set in. As stockholders frantically offered their holdings for sale, stock prices naturally went into a free fall, and the bottom went out from under the entire stock market. On Tuesday, October 29, 1929, 16,410,030 shares of stock were sold.

In many cases, fortunes were lost practically overnight. Reports of suddenly penniless men jumping from tall buildings were not unusual. As a result of the enormous loss of wealth, sales of products in stores and from farms slowed down significantly and prices began to drop precipitously.

Since there was little demand for any product not necessary for bare survival, farm and factory production was slowed significantly. Homes and farms were being foreclosed. Purchasing power was limited to bare necessities. Families relied on soup lines in order to survive. There was no welfare or other social services available. Factories were forced to cut back on production as there was very little money to buy anything other than the very basic family needs. Our family was directly and quickly impacted by the Wall Street Crash.

At an accelerated rate, neighboring men began to be laid off from their jobs. Finally, my dad was cut back to two days per week. My dad could not support the family by working only two days a week. It was decided that the only choice was to leave Detroit and return to Arlene. At that time, and through the year 1926, the family was comprised of parents Ed and Margaret, along with oldest brother, Harold, second born brother, Don, and brother Ray.

During the course of their seven years living downstate, the family resided in at least three different locations, one being Pontiac. At one point, the family lived in a rental home on Montlieu Avenue in Detroit, and that is where this writer was born, at home, on December 28, 1927.

- Chapter Two -

The Great Depression

The Wall Street Crash and the Great Depression that followed had turned life upside down for the Ed and Margaret Sprik family. The abrupt slowdown of my dad's employment, along with the loss of income from unemployed roomers and boarders, completely dislodged our family from a comfortable lifestyle.

My parents had been enjoying a fulfilling church life, and both sang in their church choir. Older brothers, Harold and Don, worked well-paying newspaper routes, and both played in their school band. My parents were proud owners of a brand new Essex sedan.

The swift economic collapse convinced Ed and Margaret that life in Detroit was no longer an option. A return to Arlene, and the support of the local church, where each had once been a member, seemed like the logical choice. Furthermore, both Margaret and Ed had many relatives in the Arlene area who might add support.

By the spring of 1931, the tentacles of the Great Depression had extended to rural America, and Arlene area farmers were not immune. Farmers affiliated with the local Christian Reformed Church found them-

Arlene Christian Reformed Church and Parsonage, c1920 (approx).

selves unable to afford a pastor's salary. Learning of our plight, the church board offered the unoccupied parsonage as a temporary refuge for our family.

The new Essex sedan was driven north to Arlene, but many of the family's personal belongings were left in Detroit. The cost of transporting all furniture and supplies was unaffordable. The parsonage, a very large residence, appeared quite barren during our stay.

Fortunately for the Ed and Margaret Sprik family, nearly all Arlene area residents lived, directly or indirectly, off the land. Large gardens, with an abundance of produce, could be found adjacent to nearly all farm homes. Milk, eggs, and home-canned food were generously donated to us. Regardless, food supply was an issue, and my mother told a story illustrating our shortage of resources during our parsonage occupancy.

The Arlene store was located directly west of the parsonage. Store owners, Alton and Hilda, were aware of our dire circumstances. Alton was an avid hunter. One day, he brought my mother a snowshoe hare (rabbit) he had shot in a nearby swamp.

My mother was fully aware that my dad, because of a Bible passage, was opposed to dining on any animal with a clawed foot. But,

Arlene Store, c1907 Caldwell Township, Missaukee, Michigan. Alton and Hilda Whipple, proprietors

my mother, apparently skeptical of that portion of scripture, was not intending to reject a supply of meat for the family.

My dad was not home at the time, so my mother dressed out the rabbit, cooked it, and served it for the family's evening meal. She told my dad it was "chicken."

Along with the rest of the family, my dad seemed to enjoy the "chicken." Although some of us knew about this act of deception, my dad never found out about the trickery. Family lips were sealed in order to protect our mother's good name. The episode clearly demonstrates the overriding power of maternal instinct.

As time went on, I came to believe that my father knew some kind of "switcheroo" was going on, but he just never said anything. That was not out of character for him. He never said much at any time. Three words was a long sentence for him. Over time, I've come to respect him as one of the "world's greatest listeners."

My only memory of Grandma Aten, my mother's mother, occurred while we lived in the parsonage. I remember standing in her kitchen and enjoying a home-baked cookie. Grandma Aten was admired for being a kind, loving individual. Although my encounter with Grandma Aten was brief, I cherish the memory of a wonderful, caring grandma. Grandma Aten passed away in 1932.

As we settled into our temporary parsonage residence, it is unlikely that anyone in the Ed and Margaret Sprik family foresaw Arlene as our residence for most of the next ten years. There was no manufacturing in the community, and farming was the primary means of income. Furthermore, except for the church parsonage, there were no houses in Arlene. It was, however, a rather bustling place.

A blacksmith shop, for shoeing horses and repairing machinery, stood across the road and north of the store. A grist mill, for grinding corn and other grains, was located just north of the blacksmith shop.

The community owned a threshing machine, along with a steel-wheeled tractor to pull and power the machine; both were housed in a building near the grist mill. An icehouse, also owned by the community, could be found directly behind the store. The community was not electrified and ice prevented food spoilage.

Arlene Store, Country School with its Belltower, c1907
Caldwell Township, Missaukee, Michigan. AD Whipple, proprietor

The Whipple Country Store sold groceries, candy, cigarettes, and other necessities. The store was connected to a cream station, where farmers could sell their weekly supply of cream, their source of income. Milk, from hand-milked cows, was processed through a cream separator, a manually operated machine into which each farmer poured raw milk. The machine separated cream from skim milk.

Arlene was also the location of the Caldwell Township Hall, which sat diagonally across from the store. The one-room Arlene Country School stood stately across from the Township Hall. Except for my second-grade year, the Arlene school became my seat of learning through seventh grade.

- Chapter Three -

Farmhouse and Schoolhouse

It is unknown as to whether Grandma Jane Sprik's failing health had anything to do with the Sprik family move back to Arlene. Nevertheless, Grandma Sprik died while we lived in the parsonage. My only memory of her is seeing her lying in her casket in her home.

She was known to be a soft-spoken, gentle person, well-liked and highly respected by all those who knew her. She had been born in the province of Groningen in the Netherlands shortly before her family immigrated to the United States. She died at sixty-nine years of age from complications of diabetes.

It was only logical, now that grandma had passed away, that our homeless family should move in with grandpa, and that is what we did. My mother quickly took over the household operation, while my dad and older brothers took over the farm chores. Times were tough, however. Prices for products from the farm dropped sharply, and there was very little money for any essentials not produced on the farm. My mother told of the time that grandpa was offered a top price of only fifteen dollars for a full grown, year-old steer, ready for market.

In addition to approximately ten milking cows, the barn held a pigsty and a section for grandpa's three horses. Two of the Percheron horses, a dappled gray and a sorrel, were used for teamwork in the fields. The other horse, somewhat smaller, was used to pull a cultivator between rows of potatoes and corn in order to tear out weeds.

The upper level of the barn was used to store hay and other animal feed. A silo, about thirty feet high, was attached to the barn and held chopped corn (silage) to feed to cattle.

Other outbuildings included a corn crib, chicken coop, and a building with wide doors for storing special equipment. My dad used the building to store the new Essex sedan. Although the Essex was new, it was a poorly engineered vehicle and continually broke down. My dad couldn't afford to keep it running, and it was finally sold for junk.

From time to time, a used car of some description would appear on the scene, but early in our stay on Grandpa Sprik's farm, horses were the source of power. In fair weather, we rode in a horse-drawn wagon. In the winter, the horses were hooked to a sleigh. During the winter, sleigh transportation could be bitterly cold, and we struggled to find enough blankets to keep us warm.

Then there was the time I was asked to accompany Grandpa Sprik on an errand, while he drove a car. Grandpa was an expert with horses, but driving a vehicle was a relatively new experience for him. Even though I was in my very early years, I was old enough to be a skeptic.

A woven wire fence stretched across the front of Grandpa Sprik's yard, and a wide, steel mesh gate could be opened or closed at the head of the driveway. As grandpa turned into the driveway, I saw that the gate was closed. Grandpa saw it at the same time, but instead of applying brakes, he frantically pulled on the steering wheel, as he would reins on horses, and loudly shouted, "WHOA, WHOA, WHOA," as we crashed into the gate.

In addition to farm work and transportation, grandpa's horses were used, in at least one case, to provide our income. Highway M-42, the main route between Manton and Lake City, was being modernized. My dad, along

Grandpa Harm Sprik's Percheron horses.

Farmhouse and Schoolhouse

with other farmers, was hired to use horses and scoops to move gravel for the road surface.

The former Harm and Jane Sprik farm is located three-quarters of a mile from the intersection of M-42 and Lucas Road (the former center of the Arlene community). Geographically, it is about five and a half miles east of Manton, and it is one-quarter of a mile south of the juncture of M-42 and LaChance Road.

Arlene is located in Missaukee County, and county- and state-owned snowplows were limited in number. M-42 and other state and federal highways were usually kept open in the winter, but side roads often remained unplowed. Since horses were the main source of power, farmers simply connected horses to a sleigh and traveled over and through the snow to church or the store.

Daily mail delivery was a special issue, however. On at least one occasion, I witnessed Joe, our mail carrier, delivering our mail while wearing skis. He had parked his vehicle on M-42 and was delivering mail from his backpack.

At the time we moved to the Sprik farm, grandpa owned a farm dog named Ned. Ned was a collie and he roamed freely around the farm. I played with Ned throughout summer days, and I think my mother liked Ned. Because of our shortage of food supplies, I was quite surprised one day to hear my mother say, "I'm going to make a pancake for Ned."

One day in early May, my mother brought me to the wooded area behind the farmhouse to pick wildflowers (the practice is now frowned upon and may be illegal). As we sauntered through the woodland, my mother identified the various wildflowers that we added to our bouquet. I was intrigued. Shortly thereafter, without my mother's knowledge, I decided that a wildflower bouquet would be a nice surprise gift for her kitchen table. Again, without my mother's knowledge and with Ned at my side, I set out for the woods. I was four years old.

Joyfully, Ned and I roamed the woodland picking beautiful lilies, adder's-tongues, and a variety of other blooms until my small hands were full. What fun! Quickly, we struck out for the farmhouse, but I was unable to find the edge of the woods. I stopped near a stump to get my bearings before giving it another effort. After walking a considerable distance, we came to a familiar location.

"This looks exactly like the stump we just left," I muttered to myself. We started again, and again ended at the same stump. "I'm lost," I said to myself, and I sat down on the ground to attempt to find a solution.

I was very concerned, but I knew enough not to panic. I sat in one place, brainstorming ways to escape the woods. Suddenly, enlightenment struck. From the deep recesses of my immature brain, the thought sprung forth that animals have an instinctive sense of direction, and Ned would be no exception. I thought, "If I can persuade Ned to go home, I can follow him out of the woods."

"Get for home!!" I yelled at Ned, mustering all the volume and fierceness I could generate. With tail between legs, Ned trotted off in what I thought was the wrong direction. I knew better than to trust my own instincts, and I ran full speed behind Ned.

Soon, we came to the edge of the woods, and the farmhouse appeared in the distance. I did not tell my mother about being lost.

Grandpa Sprik's farm was located three-quarters of a mile from the Arlene Country School. Even though I was only four years old and would not turn five until as late as December 28, 1932, my mother decided to enroll me in kindergarten in September. I soon discovered, however, that I didn't like the teacher. Consequently, not long after the school year started, I took matters into my own hands.

During a school recess, we were let out into the schoolyard to play. Instead of stopping at the playground, I just kept on walking toward our farm home. About one-quarter of a mile along M-42, I encountered the farm home of Uncle Henry and Aunt Ruby. I was hungry and decided I would stop to see if they would give me something to eat. When I knocked on the door, there was no response. That did not solve my hunger problem, so I did the next best thing.

Like most farm families of that era, the Atens did not lock doors. So, I simply walked into the house. I soon found the cupboard where bread and jelly were stored, and I fixed myself a sandwich. About half-way through the sandwich, I began to wonder, "Should I really be doing this?"

Quickly, I tidied up everything in the kitchen, making sure I left no evidence, and proceeded on my one-half mile journey home. I was afraid to tell my parents about my luncheon event, and my mother did not re-enroll me in school until the following fall.

Following the passing of Grandma Jane Sprik, Grandpa Harm had remained active on the farm. But, very early in 1933, he began to have health problems. As his illness progressed, he was diagnosed as having stomach cancer. In that era, there was no cure, and his care became my mother's responsibility. Aspirins were the only pain relievers available, and grandpa suffered mightily. He passed away on April 20, 1933.

After Grandpa Sprik's passing, our family continued to live on the Sprik farm. Obviously, a period of time was needed in order to settle the Sprik estate and find a buyer for the farm. In the meantime, our financial hardship continued, and from time to time, my dad went to Detroit to seek employment.

At one point, we accompanied my dad to Detroit, and we stayed in an apartment on Ashland Avenue. My mother hated apartment living, however, and after three months, we returned to the farm.

As I entered first grade in the Arlene school, our family's unrelenting financial hardship continued. It was hard for me to understand how schoolmates could have money for penny candy, but I was never given pennies for such a luxury. Finally, I could stand it no longer, and I devised a cunning plan.

One day, after school was dismissed, and before starting my journey home, I searched the gravel near the school until I found two penny-sized brown stones. Pocketing the stones, I walked across the road to the country store, at that time owned by Uncle Jay and Aunt Margaret Aten. As I entered the store, Aunt Margaret walked over to the candy counter to wait on me.

With two penny candy bars in hand, I accompanied Aunt Margaret to the cash register. When she extended her hand for payment, I dropped the two stones in her hand and raced for the door with Olympic speed. I didn't bother to close the door and I could hear Aunt Margaret laughing uproariously. I felt a sense of guilt, but the chocolate was delicious. Sometimes, life has trade-offs.

An event of the mid-1930s illustrates the depth of our financial hardship. One summer day, my mother sent me to the Arlene store to purchase a grocery item. I was given a coin to purchase the item and was told that there would be ten cents in change. I was instructed to be very careful on my journey back home, so that the dime would not be lost.

The merchandise was purchased, and I started for home with the dime in my pocket. When I arrived home with the store item, I reached in my pocket for the dime. It wasn't there.

Frantically, I searched again and again through other pockets, and reality finally settled in. I remembered that I had stopped to play a few times on my return from the store, and I reasoned that I must have lost the dime on one of those occasions. My mother was very upset over the loss and I felt terrible about my lack of responsibility. I realized I had jeopardized the family money supply. Something tangible would be sacrificed. I told my mother I would search for the dime.

From mid-afternoon until the summer evening sunset, I walked back and forth over the three-quarter-mile distance between the Arlene store and our farm home, searching diligently for the dime. The ten-cent coin could not be found.

One Christmas, my dad brought home a tree he had cut from our nearby property. There was no electricity, but my mother decorated the tree with icicles and ornaments she had saved from previous Christmases. On Christmas morning, we gathered around the tree to celebrate. My three brothers were still home, but there were no gifts for them under the tree. Nor were there gifts for either of our parents.

Under the tree, however, there was one package, and my name was on it. Upon opening the package, I found an Erector Set. The entire family had pooled their money and had bought this gift for the youngest in the family. I later discovered that the Erector Set had cost sixty cents.

We could see it slowly creeping west of Packingham Road. Although it was still more than one-half mile away, the flat terrain of the Arlene basin allowed us to witness the threshing machinery slowly creeping along toward the Harm Sprik farm. The tractor in front wore three-inch spikes on its rear all steel wheels. That allowed the tractor to maintain traction while climbing hills.

Except for a few federal and state highways, all roads were comprised of clay and gravel, so the tractor lugs did little permanent damage. The front tractor wheels were also made of steel.

The community threshing machine was towed behind the tractor. The tractor and threshing machine went from farm to farm, separating grain from straw. Oats were the grain of choice in Arlene as that particular grain could be ground into horse feed, as well as feed for other livestock.

Local farmers and their hired help followed the threshing machine to the appropriate farm to collect bundles of oats, or other grains, that had been processed by a grain binder. A grain binder was towed by horses. The binder cut grain stalks and tied them in bundles. Most farmers owned a binder.

Once the threshing machine was set up, farmers, with their wagons, began collecting grain bundles from fields. As grain bundles were thrown into the threshing machine, farm hands began bagging the grain, while straw from the grain bundles was blown into a separate bin. The straw would later be used for livestock bedding.

The highlight of the day, however, was the noontime dinner supplied by the farm women hosting the threshing crew at midday. The event naturally became somewhat of a cooking and baking competition, as farm women went all out to demonstrate their cooking and baking skills.

In 1917, Ed and Margaret Sprik had purchased eighty acres of property on a land contract from an Arlene farmer. Of the eighty acres, forty acres were farmland, and forty acres were woodland. The forty acres of woodland were separated from, and about one mile from, the farmland.

The land contract was nearly paid off when the Great Depression struck. In spite of all of his efforts, my dad simply was unable to earn enough money to continue land contract payments.

Only a small balance remained on the contract when my parents learned that foreclosure proceedings on their property were underway. Although I was very young, I could sense the despair and hopelessness my parents were experiencing. But just as it was announced that my parents' property would be auctioned off on the steps of the county courthouse, an unforeseen intervention occurred.

In order to stem the tide of widespread loss of family farms, President Franklin D. Roosevelt signed into law a moratorium on all foreclosures. The ensuing delay as to remaining payments allowed my oldest brothers to find employment in Detroit. They soon sent my parents the relatively small amount of money required, and the contract was paid off. Before long, the eighty acres contributed substantially to our family income.

As we continued living on the Harm and Jane Sprik farm, my parents were fully aware that, with the passing of Harm and Jane Sprik, the estate would sell the farm and we would be forced to move to another home. With that in mind, my dad began making plans to rehabilitate the dilapidated farmhouse on the forty acres of the farmland. My dad realized that a supply of water would be the first step needed for our next residence. The old windmill on the property was not working, however. (It should be noted that the area was not yet electrified.) My dad hired the local well man, seventy-year-old Samp, to help put the windmill in working order.

It was a beautiful summer day. My dad had gone off to meet Samp and begin work on our windmill. I was playing in Grandpa Sprik's yard and looking across the landscape. Because of the flat terrain in the Arlene basin, I could see the distant farm buildings surrounding the windmill about three-quarters of a mile away.

Suddenly, the quiet tranquility was interrupted by a burst of activity. Road dust was flying, as horses with wagons, as well as a couple of automobiles, raced to converge on the windmill site. Even though I was still very young, I realized that something of great consequence was taking place. I was soon to find out what it was.

Samp, along with my dad, had climbed the ladder mounted on the side of the thirty-foot tall windmill. A platform surrounded the windmill just below the working mechanism. The platform was somewhat narrow, but it allowed for two adults to maneuver around the mechanism. My dad rarely talked, so it was somewhat of a surprise when, after connecting his own safety belt, he said to Samp, "Better put on your belt."

"Naw, I've been doing this for fifty years. I don't need the belt," Samp replied.

A smooth, sturdy gin pole leaned against the windmill for safety purposes. It was in place in case of an unexpected platform collapse. Instead of crashing to the ground, men could slide to the ground down the firmly planted gin pole.

Suddenly, Samp lost his balance. As he started to fall, he was able to grab the gin pole. In his overwhelming fright, Samp gripped the gin pole so tightly he didn't slide downward. Instead, the pole became dislodged and Samp crashed thirty feet to the ground. The pole landed on top of him. The results were as expected. The shocking fatality completely changed our family trajectory. My dad never again climbed the windmill, but not for fear of height. Ed Sprik was a deeply spiritual man, and I've always thought he considered the accident as having spiritual implications.

After an aborted attempt at school as a four-year-old, I finally started kindergarten as a five-year-old. I didn't like school. The teacher made me sit in my seat and kept telling me what to do. School was boring. At home, my mother would get a book and read stories to me. Then, I could play outside until called in for a meal.

My first-grade report card indicates to me that I was not a candidate for the honor society. The first marking period shows an average of "D," as in "dog," not "D," as in "dynamo." As of the third marking period, I managed to scrape up a "B."

The Harm and Jane Sprik farm was finally sold to Jay and Margaret Aten. We were forced to take up temporary residence in a rented house in Lake City. At the end of my second-grade education in Lake City, we moved back to Arlene, and to many new adventures.

- Chapter Four -

Childhood in Arlene

After Grandma Marchien Aten passed away in 1932, Grandpa Aten became lonely. He eventually remarried a local widowed lady and relocated to her residence. Consequently, the small house he had built and occupied became vacant.

At the same time, my parents were eager to leave the house we were renting in Lake City. So, as soon as the school year was over in the spring of 1936, we moved into the Grandpa and Grandma Aten vacant house. Our rent payments were five dollars per month to Grandpa Aten and, after his death, to the Aten estate. From my point of view at the time, I was elated to get back into the openness of the outdoor world.

The Aten house was comprised of four rooms. The kitchen was wide open to the living room. Two bedrooms, with a closet between, squared off the back side of the house. A trapdoor and primitive ladder led to a Michigan basement with some shelving for storing canned goods. An unfinished and unheated shed was attached to the kitchen. My mother used it as a laundry room.

We did not have electricity, as the community of Arlene was not supplied with electrical power at that time. A kerosene lamp supplied the lighting for the house and a kerosene lantern was used for lighting the barn after sunset in the winter.

A wood-burning kitchen range, with an oven, was used for all cooking and baking. The range was also used extensively for canning food for family consumption during the winter months. The range also contained a water reservoir. The water in the reservoir was not suitable for drinking, but my mother used the hot water for laundering clothing.

The kitchen range supplied much of the heat for the house. The remainder of the heat was provided by an oval-shaped sheet metal wood-burning stove in the living room.

An upright piano stood against one wall of the living room, and a battery-operated Philco radio occupied a small table in the same room. A sofa sat against one living room wall, and a cushioned chair accompanied it.

Clinging to the living room wall was a wood-encased telephone. A speaker protruded from the front of the box, and a receiver on a cord hung on the side. Everyone in Arlene was on the same line. Each residence telephone had a distinct ring signal designated by the pattern of short and long rings. Our signal was three long rings followed by two short rings. Anyone in Arlene wishing to call the Ed and Margaret Sprik residence turned the crank on the side of their telephone accordingly. Anyone in Arlene could listen to the telephone conversation of their neighbors, and often did.

Long-distance calls were processed through a telephone switchboard operator in Lake City. Long-distance calls were rare, however, as the cost of long-distance calling was significant.

The only storage space in the house was in a very primitive attic reached by a rickety ladder. A straw tick, a mattress cover stuffed with straw, took up floor space in the attic and was rarely used.

A water pump, which supplied all our water, stood directly behind the house. It was my job to pump all the water for drinking, cooking, laundry, and for all livestock. Once a week, and usually on Saturday nights, I also pumped water for my laundry tub bath.

The small hip-roofed red barn behind the house contained two livestock stalls, a hay storage area, and a chicken coop. My dad kept his horse in one livestock stall and our Jersey cow occupied the other stall. Approximately twenty or thirty chickens were housed in the chicken coop.

A large garden plot took up space directly behind and somewhat north of the barn. And, of course, there was the out back two-holer.

There was little need for wallpaper in my bedroom. I was a sports fanatic from an early age, and my bedroom walls were covered from floor to ceiling with newspaper photos of my baseball and football heroes.

Since we did not have electricity, we had no way to keep meat. My mother likely would have canned beef if it were available. We did not have funds for such a luxury, however, so eggs became our source of protein. Chickens were a very inexpensive resource, as they were free ranged throughout our yard and nearby fields through spring, summer, and fall. Relatives and neighbors brought some of their surplus corn from time to time, and once a day, we threw corn out for the chickens. Eggs were not the only source of protein from the chickens, however.

Once a year, my mother usually ordered a supply of straight run chicks from a hatchery. Half the chicks would, naturally, turn out to be roosters. As the hens became old enough to begin laying eggs, the roosters became just right for Sunday dinners. My dad did not want to be the executioner of the roosters, so the job fell to the next in line. I didn't like the job, either, but mine was not to choose. I developed a system of selecting which rooster qualified for the upcoming Sunday dinner.

During nice weather, I was usually out in the yard with no shirt, no shoes, and nothing but a pair of cutoffs. As roosters get older, they can get obnoxiously mean. As I played in the yard, a rooster would sometimes sneak up behind me and spur me with his sharp leg spikes in the back of my legs. Quickly, I would turn and identify that rooster by a mark of some kind. That would be the next weekend feast.

From time to time, my older brothers brought used cars from Detroit to our Arlene home for my dad to sell. These cars were bought at wholesale prices in Detroit and could be sold by my dad for a decent profit. One such vehicle was a one-seat coupe with a rumble seat. When my parents drove to Lake City or Manton, I rode in the rumble seat. But my mother didn't drive, and when my dad went off to work, my mother didn't have transportation to ladies' church events. A particularly important women's event was scheduled to take place at a home about two miles distant. My mother was insistent on being there, and my dad couldn't take off work.

My dad had shown me how to drive the various vehicles appearing in our yard from time to time, and the rumble-seated coupe was one of those vehicles. On the evening prior to my mother's special event, my dad instructed me to drive slowly and carefully. Some life experiences are simply unforgettable. This was one of them.

With my mother at my side, I carefully and cautiously drove the two miles to our destination and then drove home. When it was time to pick up my mother, I went out to the coupe, started the motor, and took off down the road. After I returned home with my mother, I began to realize how fortunate I was, because I might have encountered a police officer. In order to receive a driver's license, a person needed to be fourteen years old. I was only seven.

Ed Sprik was raised by an abusive and exploitive father. Although he had no role model, my dad tried to be a good parent. A couple times each summer, he would accompany me to a lake for a swim. On one of those occasions, he taught me how to dog paddle.

In order for a rural household to move forward, everyone in the family needed to work cooperatively. That being said, I had a role to play in our family as to chores that needed to be done, some on a daily basis. One of those ongoing, year-round chores was splitting firewood.

My dad cut the firewood from our forty-acre parcel and both a neighbor and I, along with my dad, cut the logs into proper lengths with a crosscut saw. It was my job, however, to then split the wood, on a daily basis, for both the sheet metal stove and for the kitchen range. My dad showed me how to safely split the wood with my foot propped against a block for stability. While other boys would occasionally show up at school with a cut on their foot, I remained uninjured. That was due to my dad's superior skills from his logging camp days.

Milking our Jersey cow by hand every evening was another of my daily chores. My dad milked the cow every morning. As milk was brought in from the barn, it was divided into two separate containers. One container held the milk used for cereal and for cooking. The milk in the other container was allowed to sit for a day or two until the cream rose to the top. At that point, some cream would be skimmed off for coffee cream. The remaining cream was allowed to accumulate for several days until there was a sufficient amount to be churned into butter.

I was tasked with gathering eggs most days. In addition, I was also required to scatter corn around the yard once a day when the chickens were free ranging.

Other than working in the garden, there was no work I hated like picking berries. My hands are big and strong but not suitable for picking small huckleberries. Furthermore, the weather was hot, and there was little shade. My mother was very good at finding and picking berries, however. Blueberries were canned and used for delicious desserts throughout the fall and winter. So, how did we slake our thirst while spending long days in the berry patch? Water would become warm and undrinkable. My mother simply added tea leaves to the water in the jar, and we would then drink tea.

In addition to canning berries, my mother made fruit into jam. She also bought peaches and pears and canned them on the kitchen range. Apples were often picked from abandoned orchards. My mother knew

Childhood in Arlene

most of the landowners in the area, and usually a simple telephone call would give us access. The apples were uncultured, but the bad parts of the fruit were cut out before canning. Along with the wild berries, apples were free food for our family. Also, our large garden supplied much of our food through the summer and fall.

I'm fronting the family at our Arlene home.
L to R: brother Ray, mother Margaret, brother Harold, father Ed, brother Don (behind camera).

Butter was relatively inexpensive, and sometimes my mother bought it from the store. Other times, we made our own butter. The accumulated cream from our milkings was placed in a two-quart fruit jar. The jar was then shaken back and forth until the butter separated from the buttermilk. Water was then squeezed from the butter and salt was added. The buttermilk, however, was a different matter.

I had sampled buttermilk earlier, and I couldn't stand the taste of it. My dad had somehow developed a taste for it, however. In fact, he acted as if it was a rare treat, and he gulped down the entire bottle each time we churned butter. He also loved Limburger cheese.

I awoke one day while my mother was fixing my dad's lunch. The odor was new to me, but it was not easily forgotten. As the lunch bucket closed, I heard my mother make the understatement of the decade. "Ed, I wish you would buy something else for your sandwiches."

A red wagon bought for me by older brothers Harold and Don proved to be my most useful toy. I pulled the wagon to the community icehouse, broke out an ice block, and towed the ice home. This chore took place during spring and summer. As the fall season came on, the ice supply would be exhausted. At that point, food preservation became a big problem.

The icehouse was located directly behind the Arlene store. Each winter, men from the community gathered at nearby Poll's Lake with their horses and sleighs. An ice saw was used to cut the blocks of ice, which were then loaded onto the sleighs.

Sawdust was used to separate the individual blocks of ice and to provide insulation. Ice was taken from the icehouse by members of the community on the honor system. Obviously, from a practical standpoint, there was no need to take more ice than was needed, as the extra ice would simply melt.

Except for my second-grade year, my entire formal kindergarten through seventh-grade education was acquired at the one-room Arlene Country School. The term "formal" is used because an Encyclopedia Britannica set occupied a shelf in our home, and I could often be found holding a book from that shelf.

The Arlene school was a well-built, red brick building which, to this day, is used as the Caldwell Township Hall. A tower housing a school bell stood above the entrance. A rope hanging down in the entrance activated the bell. The bell was used to signal the start of the school day. It also signaled the termination of recesses and lunch breaks.

A teacher's desk, a lengthy recitation bench, and a wall-mounted chalkboard occupied the front of the school. Bathrooms, one for the girls and one for the boys, were located on each side of the doorway. Each contained a chemical toilet and washstand.

Seats, each with a writing platform, were distributed throughout the building, with seats for older students occupying the back of the room. The building was heated by a coal furnace located in the basement.

Except for the fifth- and sixth-grade years, I experienced a different teacher each year. Other than Mrs. Long, my seventh-grade teacher, I did not relate well to any of my teachers. In some cases, I actually disliked them. That was because I was always sort of a rebel. In one case, in which my best friend was unfairly physically punished, I almost did the unthinkable. I came within a hair's breadth of rising from my seat and physically attacking the male teacher.

School did not start until nine o'clock in the morning, and we were dismissed at four o'clock in the afternoon. Those hours were established to allow children to walk to and from school in daylight. Some children walked as far as two miles back and forth from home to school.

Lunch breaks were of sixty minutes duration. That allowed us to quickly devour the contents of our lunch pails and then play for the remainder of the lunch hour. During warm weather, we played softball in the schoolyard and other games during recesses. Winter noon hours were reserved for sledding on the hill behind the school. The hill was actually a part of what is now known as Lucas Road. We towed our sleds to school each school day and shared with those who didn't have sleds or lived too far away to bring sleds to school.

There were six people in my class, which was a high number for a country school, and most of them were bright, shining academic stars. Naturally, our teachers were attracted to those students and they were looked upon with favor. I was not one of them, however. I believe I was looked upon by the teachers as sort of an academic "klutz," slow to accomplish tasks and mediocre in brain power. But, beginning in fifth grade, I had an opportunity to "even the score."

On Friday afternoons, at the end of the school week, teachers often conducted a spelldown in which all upper grades participated. Teachers usually provided an inexpensive prize for the winner. Although I was slow and somewhat laborious in other schoolwork, I was an excellent speller. As the various three- and four-syllable words were presented, one by one the academic stars began to tumble, until I was the only one standing. Week after week, no one could beat me. Without exception, I won every spelldown. Prizes, however, were of questionable value. Once, I received a bow tie.

Report cards of my early school days present me as a very average student, at best. Math was always difficult for me, but I did better in subjects such as geography and reading, and, of course, spelling.

Not blessed with an outstanding voice, my mother would, nevertheless, sing to me. These songs were referred to as "ditties," but I emulated my mother. Thus began my interest in music, my ability to "carry a tune," and my sense of pitch. This musical ability quickly became apparent to teachers when I was in early grades.

At the beginning of each school day, our teacher handed out yellow, paper-backed songbooks that were specifically written for elementary grade children. For about fifteen minutes, thereafter, the teacher led us in singing. Apparently, my voice stood out from others. Each year, as the time for the all-school Christmas program approached, the teacher would tell me that I would perform the solo part.

I never could figure out why I was selected for the role, and I looked ahead to the Christmas program with dread and anxiety. But, as much as I disliked being the school soloist, there was one Christmas event that I look back on with a sense of considerable achievement.

I was asked, no told, that for that particular program, I was to perform the Latin version of "O Come, All Ye Faithful." I objected, but unsuccessfully. Following significant after-school coaching by the teacher, who had completed two years of high school Latin, and with diligent practice at home, I mounted the makeshift stage, fearing the worst. My hard work paid off, however, and I sang "Adeste Fideles" flawlessly. Although I didn't realize it at the time, the door had been opened to a lifetime of rich musical experiences.

Throughout those years in the Aten house, religion permeated our lives. We were required to attend catechism classes each and every Saturday morning. Sunday School took place after the Sunday afternoon services. At home, we were required to study Sunday School lessons and catechism lessons so as to be properly prepared for the classes to follow.

The Arlene Christian Reformed Church was not electrically lighted, and the denominational synod required each church under its control to hold two full-blown services each Sunday. Consequently, Dutch language service was conducted at 10 a.m. and an English service at 2 p.m. Later, the morning Dutch service was changed to English. To my everlasting gratitude, my parents did not require me to attend the morning service. The drawn-out sermons did provide a benefit for the local farmers, however, as after a scrumptious and filling dinner, they could catch a decent nap.

Sunday was the day of the week my school chums and I dreaded. Furthermore, the long-winded sermons never seemed to cure much of the sinfulness of my peers. Freddie Poll continued to kick everybody's shins with steel-toed, high-top boots during recess soccer games, and Barney D couldn't get to the back of the schoolhouse quick enough, during lunch hour, in order to roll himself a corn-silk cigarette. But there was some good that came from it all.

It was after sitting restlessly in our church pew all those long hours, week after week, hearing long and profound sermons, that I finally learned how to wiggle my ears.

Throughout my grade school years, I was forced to deal with abscessed teeth. When a tooth started to decay, the side of my face would always balloon out and the accompanying pain was severe. My mother tried home remedies, none of which worked. But I was not taken to a dentist. This ordeal continually repeated itself. At the time, I reasoned that the fifty-cent extraction fee was not affordable for my parents. Later, I came to the realization that my parents' monthly contribution to the church collection plate might better have been used for my dental care.

Except for smallpox, for which all school children had been vaccinated, childhood communicable diseases continued to run rampant through elementary-age children. Chicken pox, red measles, German measles, and mumps all made their way through the Arlene school. Polio took the life of our schoolmate, Chrystal Whipple. Scarlet fever was one of the most dangerous of the epidemics to hit Arlene. Its tentacles reached out to the Arlene adult population as well. Farmer, George Kleinheksel, a close neighbor, along with Liz Vander Weide, a mother of small children, came down with the disease, and both nearly succumbed. A prayer vigil was held. As more and more children came down with the disease, I also became a victim.

For more than four weeks, I was bedridden with a high fever and chills. The county health department posted our house, indicating we were quarantined in. Only my dad was allowed to leave the house, and it is possible groceries were brought to him outside the store building when we needed supplies.

During a follow-up visit with Dr. Holm, I was told I was not to run or play any sports for a calendar year. A stethoscope test had indicated that scarlet fever had left me with a heart murmur.

Time was needed for the heart damage to heal. It was a tough pill to swallow for an athletically inclined eleven-year-old boy. As difficult as it was, however, I religiously followed the doctor's advice, out of fear of additional heart damage.

Throughout grade school and high school, I was plagued with a right-side hernia. While playing in the schoolyard during recess of my second-grade year, the hernia popped out through the tear in my lower abdominal sheath and the hernia strangulated.

I was alone on the playground at the time, and there was no one to help me. With intense pain, I struggled the two blocks to our rented house in Lake City. Fortunately, my mother was home. She tried to put the hernia back in place but to no avail. We had no transportation, so it was decided that we had no choice other than to walk three blocks to the doctor's office.

Immediately, the physician sedated me with chloroform and put the hernia in place. As I proceeded through junior high and high school athletics, the hernia continued to cause problems. Out of necessity, however, I learned how to inconspicuously put the hernia back in place, even when playing before spectators. From time to time, my mother bought trusses and various other contraptions, in an effort to control the hernia. Throughout my struggles with the hernia, however, surgery was never discussed, undoubtedly due to costs.

Shortly after returning to Arlene from Lake City, I witnessed a small gymnasium being built. It was attached to the rear of the Arlene school. A heating duct was installed and connected to the school furnace. A backboard and rim with net were put up on each end of the gym. Construction was funded by a federal grant.

For lighting, Alton Whipple, owner of the Arlene store, along with his wife, Hilda, extended wiring from the electric generator in his store to the gym. In various ways, the gymnasium became a social and recreational center for the entire community.

Alton Whipple had played basketball at Manton High School, and he soon organized independent basketball teams. Players were comprised of younger men in the community. Games were scheduled against Jennings, Camp Axin (CCC Camp), and occasionally against Manton and Lake City. Alton was an important part of the team and he also was the manager. He also was of large body and didn't hesitate to intimidate. He "didn't take prisoners" either.

On one occasion, he scheduled a game with Lake City. On game day, the Lake City manager called Alton asking for a postponement because he had accidently scheduled another game for that exact date. Alton refused to postpone the game, and the Lake City team was substantially weakened by dividing itself into two separate units. The Arlene team naturally prevailed against a cobbled-up Lake City team, and Alton made sure everyone coming into the store heard about "Arlene beating Lake City!"

On Wednesday nights, during the winter, the gym was reserved for men's volleyball. My dad often participated. Ladies Aid Sales took place in the gym periodically. Quilts, and other handmade dry goods, sewn by members of the Arlene church, were auctioned off. Proceeds went to mission projects. My dad, along with George Kleinheksel, always clerked the sales, and Uncle Henry Aten served as auctioneer. Uncle Ralph Aten sometimes assisted with auctioneering. The once-a-month community parties were, however, the social highlights of the year.

On those special evenings, the festivities usually started with poetry or other readings and sometimes a musical presentation. Next, a time would be set aside for good, old-fashioned folk dancing. Since accompanying musical instruments were not available, dancers sang the music as well as the lyrics. The evening was capped off with tables of homemade pies, cakes, and volumes of other delicious foods brought in by women of the community.

Most of the time, the gymnasium door remained unlocked, and a basketball could be found lying somewhere on the floor. As often as possible, particularly during winter months, my cousin Ray Aten and I shot baskets during recesses and lunch hours. Later, this activity would have special significance.

I don't recall having many pets during our stay at the Aten house, but I'll never forget one that was covered with feathers. My parents were visiting at the home of a Helsel family near Lake City. During the course of the evening, I noticed a black bird strolling around the yard. To my surprise, the bird approached me, and I began to play with my new feathered friend. Mrs. Helsel took note of my attraction to the feathered creature and suggested I take it home with me as a pet.

The summer night was as black as coal and there wasn't a sound in the air as Uncle Henry strode cautiously down the narrow trail road leading to our old farmhouse. Slowly and carefully, he turned off the road and with arms outstretched, began to feel for the fence that separated our house from the road. At last, he found the gate, opened it, and started through the narrow opening.

As my uncle's right ear passed the six-foot high gatepost, my pet crow, Blackie, decided he had waited long enough. Sitting atop the post and completely blending in with the dark of the night, Blackie let loose with his hair-raising cry of alarm—CAWWWWW!!! The raspy blast from the throat of my black-feathered pet split the night air and nearly launched my unsuspecting uncle into orbit.

Blackie lived with us for only one summer, but during that time, he established himself as one of my most memorable pets. He became particularly adept at crowing like the barnyard roosters and his imitations of our barking dog became amazingly realistic. His favorite pastime was to sit on top of my outstretched dog during sunny afternoons and explore for the ever-present fleas that pestered the little dog. Blackie's unbeliev-able vision became apparent to me as I watched him unerringly seek out and eat the microscopic fleas that hid in the little dog's heavy coat of hair. Oddly, the dog did not object, and as the summer wore on, a strong alliance developed between them. Blackie disappeared one day, and I have never known what happened to him. I only know that he added a touch of brightness to one summer for a nine-year-old boy.

It was a time of small farms and large gardens. As we wended our way through the elementary grades in our country school, summer vacations were not work-free times in our lives. When we did get free time, it seldom occurred simultaneously with free time of others in the Arlene vicinity. Consequently, most of my summers were spent by my-self, figuring out my own entertainment activities.

But one day, my older brothers arrived from Detroit for the week-end bringing with them a small pug-nosed, tail-wagging, short-legged brown dog, mostly Pekingese, but also of other mixed ancestry. He had been lodged in a Detroit "dog pound (impoundment)," now known as an animal shelter. Although he was a happy little dog, we soon discovered he had another side to his personality.

He was a feisty, fearless rascal, willing to take on any dog even four times his size that dared enter our yard. He also would bite. Not out of meanness, but only when he saw someone pick up an item to take with them, regardless of ownership. Once, to our extreme embarrassment, he bit our church pastor when he picked up his hat to leave. Once, a neighbor kicked at him upon entering our yard. A battle ensued, and from then on, there was all-out war whenever that neighbor appeared on the scene. Brownie was not one to back down. He was my constant companion.

Brownie was in the house during winters, but he rarely left my side for several memorable summers. Together, we roamed the fields and woods of the general vicinity. And my attachment to my little companion became intense, to say the least.

As was nearly always the case during that era and in rural areas, pets, many of them working dogs, were allowed to run free. In Brownie's case, he was let out each morning, at which time he would tour the neighborhood farmyards in a predictable circuitous route. We soon came to realize he was a flagrant Romeo, always seeking more than a bit of romance. But, alas, self-indulgent behavior was his undoing.

It was late fall, just past 9 a.m. The school bell had just rung, and before serious studying began, it was time for "show and tell." A young student was in front of the room to take his turn. "Brownie got hit by a car and is dead beside the road," he blurted.

This kid needs a haircut! Brownie could use one too. And who is going to split all this wood? Don't child labor laws apply?

I was horrified. I had never before experienced such total loss, devastation, and shock. My world was pulled from beneath my feet. I leaped from my seat and lunged for the door. Frantic, and beside myself with grief, I raced the one-eighth-mile distance to my house and burst through the door into our kitchen, and into my mother's arms, desperately grasping for a nonexistent untruth of the total situation.

To this day I do not know why they are called BB guns. But at seven years of age, I received my first one, a single shot, as I remember, and it came as a Christmas gift. We lived in town at the time so there was little chance to use it. But we soon moved back to the country, and the BB gun was soon put into use.

But my older brothers soon decided to upgrade my weaponry and from them, I received a beautiful copper coated lever action repeater model. It was my pride and joy. I had the sharpest looking BB gun in the neighborhood. A tube of one hundred BBs cost five cents at the Arlene store.

When ammunition was available, my targets were knots in fence posts, tin cans set on posts, and above all sparrows and starlings. It was great sport trying to hit them while they were flying, but I was never successful in doing so. Robins were considered sacred, and I was told never to shoot one. I didn't.

My mother continually warned me of the danger involved in owning and using a BB gun. My mother actually hated guns and was afraid of them. She often reminded me of the responsibility of gun ownership. She told me, and it was true, that I could put out someone's eye with a BB gun. She told me never to shoot at anyone in anyway whatsoever. Later in life, as I considered her fear of guns, I wondered why she allowed me to even have a BB gun.

But, one day while playing with a neighbor friend, I was accidently struck on a pant leg by a stray pellet. The BB had been fired from considerable distance, so its momentum had waned. Furthermore, the loose hanging fabric absorbed the force of the BB and I barely felt the impact. From that experience, I drew a very inaccurate conclusion.

Ignoring the fact that my mother was a particularly wise, intelligent individual, I reasoned that a pellet fired from a BB gun could not hurt a person wearing overall pants (blue jeans as they are now called).

My immature logic convinced me that my mother didn't understand BB guns. In order to prove my hypothesis, I told my visiting cousin to shoot me in the rear with my copper coated BB model. He knew this was wrong, and he absolutely did not want to do it. But I insisted. My mental flaw was in bending slightly forward, so instead of hanging loosely, my trousers tightened against my skin.

Many incidents of my grade school days have long been forgotten. But a few events were so totally impressive when it came to life in general, and BB guns in particular, that they are deeply engraved in my conscience. This escapade was one of them. It was not the shot heard 'round the world, but it could very well have been the "Y-O-W-L" heard 'round Arlene. It stung like a thousand bees and without letup. My cousin, now beside himself with guilt, apologized nonstop.

The pain was beyond the crying stage. My mother came rushing out of the house to survey the damage. The pellet didn't penetrate the skin but sitting down was unthinkable. But, if there was any redemption, whatsoever, for my inexcusable stupidity, it was the fact that the dreadful consequences of my disobedience made any punishment totally out of the question.

One evening, as we sat comfortably in our Arlene living room, my dad pulled a harmonica from his pocket and began to play. Not only that, he played with an advanced rhythmic beat that seemed to light up the room. I was stunned. He had never mentioned his harmonica playing. He continued playing a variety of tunes and wound up the evening with a speedy polka number. I was intrigued and asked my dad to teach me how to play the instrument.

Soon, he taught me how to hold the instrument (I later learned it was a left-handed version) and suggested I start by learning to play "Silent Night." Diligently, and day after day, I sat on our front porch steps trying to learn the first musical phrase of that Christmas carol. Once I learned to play the first line of the song, the remainder of "Silent Night" fell into place. My next challenge was a western song entitled "Cowboy Jack." I was surprised at how quickly I could learn it.

Along the way, my dad taught me an advanced technique called "tonguing." With that method of playing, I could add a rhythmic beat to my music, and it made playing, as well as listening, much more interesting.

Other than splitting wood, working in the garden, and the daily milking, my time was pretty much unstructured. Unless I was assigned to picking berries, apples, or cherries, much of my time was taken up roaming and exploring the vast area south of our house. Abandoned houses were among my favorite places. Immigrants had purchased cheap land after it had been logged off. The severe northern winters and their lack of knowledge as to farming soon drove them back to cities. Homes were simply abandoned.

As difficult as it was to make a living, my parents always saw fit to subscribe to a daily newspaper. They also subscribed to the *Manton Tribune Record*, a weekly, and to the *Missaukee Republican* from time to time when they could afford it. I read the sports pages cover to cover, and I idolized baseball stars. Professional football was just getting underway, and professional basketball had not yet arrived on the scene. As much as I enjoyed sports, I seldom had a playmate to share a game. Sometimes, I improvised.

Repeatedly, I often tossed a ball up on the barn roof so that I could attempt to catch it as it was ejected from the flanged roof. As time went on, I became adept and the flying objects seldom escaped my grasp.

On one Christmas morning, I received a bicycle from my oldest brothers. I often rode it back and forth to the Arlene country store, but the bike was of little use to me on loose gravel roads of the area. I was the only person in the area owning a bicycle. On one occasion, a schoolmate called me on the telephone to ask if he could take a ride on my bike.

Showing off the only bike in Arlene.

After showing him how to work the pedals and how to steer, I allowed him to ride back and forth to the store a few times. After ten or fifteen minutes of riding, he thanked me profusely and then proceeded to walk the two miles back to his home.

Regardless of the stifling economy of the 1930s, it could be hard to find a farmstead that did not house a sled. Most of them displayed the trademark American Flyer. In addition to their use during lunch breaks on school days, sleds were towed by neighborhood children to the steep hills directly south of our house on Saturdays. Time after time, we pulled sleds back up the steep hills after a breathtaking ride to the bottom. Sometimes, boys and girls raced each other down the hill. Owning a fast sled was considered quite an honor. On bitter cold Saturdays or during Christmas vacations, I might be the only person to brave the elements in order to get in an afternoon of sledding. I sometimes paid a significant price for those outings, however, as the warming of my hands and feet in front of the stove upon my return home was an exceedingly painful process.

During the 1930s, there was little traffic on rural highways. Frequently, while we were alone in the truck, my dad would move to the passenger seat and allow me to drive. Over time, I became quite competent and even learned how to operate the hydraulic lift. As a driver, I became very efficient with the various vehicle controls, largely due to the fact that I was my mother's chauffeur. My mother feared getting behind the wheel. Consequently, while my dad was at work, I was the only resource available for transportation to berry patches and apple orchards, as well as the aforementioned ladies' church events. I was far too young for a driver's license, however, and we simply ignored the law. I greatly enjoyed driving, and one day a special opportunity presented itself.

It was a Sunday morning, and my parents had dutifully gone off to church. It was a beautiful summer morning and instead of driving the truck, our only means of transportation at the time, my parents decided to walk the short distance to the church. I checked the truck's controls. The keys were in the ignition.

Throughout my life, I have been somewhat resentful of authority. By and large, however, I have always tried to be respectful. For a period of time, I debated the issue, but, during a moment of moral weakness, I jumped behind the steering wheel, fired up the engine, and drove out through the gate. I knew better than to drive out on the main road, so I turned right and drove back and forth over the quarter-mile distance to the sledding hill. My sense of guilt was really bearing down on me, but I was overwhelmed by the joyfulness I was experiencing. While church service was still in session, I pulled the truck back into the yard to what I thought was the exact location it had been sitting. I turned off the engine and returned to the house, awaiting my parents' return.

My parents never told me how they found out about my unauthorized expedition, but after a "mandatory" warning, the incident was never again discussed.

After his death from cancer, Grandpa Sprik's farm had been sold to Uncle Jay Aten, my mother's brother. We lived about a mile away, but I sometimes went there to play with my cousin, Jay Aten Jr. Uncle Jay's wife, Margaret, was an avid reader, and there were large stacks of magazines and newspapers, in a number of places, around the premises. On quiet afternoons, when we weren't needed for work, we spent hours perusing various periodicals, searching for coupons that offered free stuff. However, I don't remember ever receiving anything.

But Junior, as we called him, a name he later came to hate, was four years older than I was, and I do believe he thought it was his obligation to lead us to various types of adventures. His judgment was often flawed, however, and I should have been more cautious when he asked me if I wanted to take some airplane rides. Apprehensive as I was regarding my cousin's judgment, I had been intrigued by the one airplane that had flown over our house that summer. The idea of flying through space was irresistible.

Junior led us to a steep bank that dropped off directly behind the red barn. I didn't see any wings or propeller, but my cousin quickly explained that we didn't need any. Lying on his back at the top of the steep slope, with his knees tucked against his chest, Junior advised me to sit on his feet so he could propel me upward and over the edge of the drop-off. Upon so doing, I suddenly found myself airborne as if being projected upward and outward by some type of spring-loaded device. The euphoric airborne sensation was one I had never before experienced. I couldn't wait to get back to the top of the slope to try it again.

Loading the human slingshot again with me as the projectile, Junior decided to give me an even more exciting space flight by adding all the thrust he could muster. But, alas, his enthusiasm was offset by physical coordination problems, and instead of thrusting upward, he forcefully shoved outward with all the power he could generate. This resulted in a counter-clockwise rotation of my body, and I have a memory of slamming down on the ground on my back with arms and legs extended upward.

The physical experience that took place was one I had never before known. I struggled to my feet, but the earth seemed to have lost its oxygen wrap. Wild-eyed and panicked beyond imagination, with deflated lungs, I could not speak. I could not cry. I could not breathe. I seriously considered that I might be forever leaving this planet. As my breathing eventually returned, I came to the decision that future airplane rides would be in a licensed flying machine.

During a seven-year span, the Ed and Margaret Sprik family experienced almost unbearable grief and sadness. From 1931 through 1937, five family members passed away:

> Jane (Brink) Sprik – April 20, 1862, to May 10, 1931
>
> Marchien (Meijer) Aten – 1857 to 1932
>
> Harm Sprik – May 3, 1861, to April 20, 1933
>
> Jacob Aten – 1857 to 1935
>
> Ray Sprik – 1918 to 1937

Several years ago, I opened the deer season in Arlene, where we still own the forty acres of woodland that were purchased by my parents in 1917. As I stood on a high hill overlooking the basin that cradles this tiny community, I thought about the old folks that are now gone, many of their homes still standing and, in most cases, occupied by strangers.

The Arlene store burned to the ground, and the old church has been torn down. The country school has been painted white and now serves as the township hall. The old school gym rotted away and had to be demolished.

But thankfully, Arlene has not become a community of tourism, glitz, and glitter. The community still produces and creates wealth. Instead of hay fields and potato vines, however, one now sees hundreds of thousands of Christmas trees covering the land.

- Chapter Five -

Sports, Music, and ... War

As we sat in the living room of our rented four-room Arlene home, the voice on our battery-operated radio was unexpectedly interrupted by a knock on our front door. As my mother opened the door, she was met by a well-dressed man in a suit and tie. He introduced himself as a Mr. Kruger, representing a wholesale potato firm with warehouses throughout the area.

After the usual cordialities, Mr. Kruger invited my dad to join his firm as the manager of a Manton, Michigan, potato warehouse. Mr. Kruger informed us that he was seeking a person with a background in the business field. He said he had learned that, several years earlier, my dad and mother had owned and operated a general store in Manton. He believed my dad would be a very good fit for management of their Manton warehouse. Characteristically, my dad did not respond.

As he made his way to the door, Mr. Kruger asked my dad to give the matter consideration. It's not clear, at this time, as to whether or not there was a response deadline. My dad agreed to give it some thought.

At the time of Mr. Kruger's visit, my dad owned a relatively new Ford dump truck. Road construction was underway throughout the general area, and my dad was able to work steadily on the various road projects. Income was sparse during the coldest months, however, and my dad's summer income had to carry us through the winter months. After due consideration, my dad decided to sell his truck and take the warehouse management position. We moved to a rental house in Manton.

Our house in Manton was an enormous upgrade from our Arlene house. We suddenly had electric power, running water, an indoor bathroom with tub, and a coal furnace. Upon moving in, I went throughout the house flipping light switches.

I liked living in Manton because it was a blue-collar town, although I didn't really think about that when I was a teenager. But I was accepted into the community, as were other farm kids, who came into town from other farms and country schools.

My eighth-grade year in Manton was pretty much a review of what I had already learned, as we were quite advanced in our Arlene Country School.

In Manton High School baseball uniform as a sophomore.

Manton did not have a football team, so we played fall baseball against other schools who did not field football teams. There were many schools whose athletic programs consisted of only boys' baseball and basketball. A few schools also fielded girls' basketball teams. I was a starter on the baseball team as a freshman, only because most players had graduated the previous year. I was a good fielder but not a very good hitter.

I also played on the eighth-grade basketball team but was not very good. I went out for basketball as a ninth-grader but did not make a single field goal or free throw the entire season. Near the end of the season, I spent most of my time on the bench. But between May of my ninth-grade year and October of the same year, my body went through an immense physical change. From about a five-foot-nine, pudgy, uncoordinated kid, I emerged as a six-foot-one, rangy, muscular individual. Within six months, I suddenly became one of the best boxers, one of the fastest runners, and one of the best high jumpers in the entire high school. As an example of the sudden change, an obstacle course had been set up behind the high school. A flat wall, about seven feet high, was one of the challenges. While other boys leaped up, grabbed the top and scrambled over, I would barely be able to reach the top, then flail away with my legs, unable to make any progress at all. I was humiliated by my ineptitude.

But several weeks later, I went out to the wall, leaped up, grabbed the top and practically flew over the wall. I was astounded.

Although I was not aware of it at the time, a vision issue hampered my high school athletic career. This disability affected my hitting in base-ball and my long-range shooting in basketball. Much later, when I was an adult, the problem was discovered and corrected with prescription glasses. Nevertheless, my size, strength, and speed counteracted my vision issues, to a large extent.

Throughout high school, my life centered around sports and music. I played clarinet in the high school band through twelfth grade and often played snare drums, bass drums, or cymbals in marching band. Because of a shortage of teachers during World War II, our band teacher taught English classes, except for the two class periods each day when he directed middle school and high school band. As I

Music became a big part of my life in Manton High School.

recall, teachers did not have a prep time. Consequently, our band program was very weak, to say the least.

While in my junior and senior years, I bowled at the local bowling alley on a team named "the Squirts." We bowled in the regular men's league and held our own pretty well. The team was comprised of Russ and Jerry Allen, Dan Cook, Bob Cunningham, and me. Mrs. Allen sewed the team's name on a white T-shirt for each of us. We were proud of our fancy "uniforms."

Saturday night was usually "bowling alley" night for many of us. Fifty cents would allow for two bowling games and a ten-cent ice cream sundae. If we could find any nickels, we could play the jukebox to listen and dance to the Guy Lombardo, Glenn Miller, and Artie Shaw bands. Somehow, as a group, we were usually able to keep the jukebox going until closing time.

Men walk backward digging potatoes with forks for one dollar per day. Young people followed the diggers, gathering potatoes into bushel-sized crates for 2¢ a bushel.

Meanwhile, during potato vacation, I worked for my dad in the potato warehouse he managed. As was common practice throughout rural northern Michigan, schools were closed for two weeks in October to allow students to pick up potatoes for area farmers. Potato harvesting machines were not yet available, and student labor was the only means of getting the crop to market.

Farmers often paid unemployed men approximately one dollar a day for digging potatoes with a fork. Students followed behind them, picking up potatoes for two cents per bushel. The income was important to young people, who often needed the money to buy school clothes.

After two years as manager of the potato warehouse, my dad decided to start a small farm machinery and used car business. Property was purchased on the north end of Manton, and my dad soon acquired an Allis-Chalmers and New Idea franchise. He hired two mechanics and a bookkeeper. The business flourished. In the meantime, we moved to the north end of Manton.

To my dad, his business was his pleasure. Because of his earlier farm background, he simply relished talking with

Ed Sprik stands in front of his Manton farm machinery business in the mid-1940s.

the farmers who stopped in. One day, however, he said to my mother and me, "Other people take vacations. Maybe we should take a vacation. I'll rent a cottage for three days."

We discovered that a boat went with the cottage rental. So, the next morning, my mother, dad, and I headed for the nearby lake with cane fishing poles and a can of worms. Fish were not biting and after a period of time, my dad pulled out his pocket watch to check the time. Shortly thereafter, he again pulled his watch to check the time. Intervals between time checks became shorter and shorter until my dad made an announcement. "Frank Thompson might be stopping in today to talk about a hay baler. I better get over to the business place in case he shows up." For the next two days, he appeared at the cottage only for the evening meal and to sleep.

During my youthful days in Manton, I involved myself in some really thoughtless adventures. But the highlight of this brainless activity took place on one sunny summer day when there was absolutely nothing to gain from my pea-brained escapade. While driving one of our used cars, I approached the heavily used railroad tracks running through the center of Manton.

Carefully lining up my wheels and looking north and south for an approaching train, I decided to drive the car on the train tracks through the downtown park and to the next intersection. A lot of people would think this was not a very good idea. By the luckiest of circumstances, the outside of my car tires fit perfectly against the inside of the rails.

As I drove through the park, I opened the driver's side window and waved to the people sitting on the veranda of the nearby Pier Hotel. I don't remember them returning my wave. At the next intersection, I pulled up on the road. I deliberately avoided thinking of the possible consequences if my tires had become tightly wedged between the rails.

Throughout grade school and high school, I was a sports fanatic. I listened to broadcasts of Detroit Tigers baseball whenever possible. Somehow, I was able to save enough money for a subscription to *Sporting News* magazine, a publication that regularly reported statistics on every aspect of professional baseball, including the minor leagues. I consistently read it from cover to cover and was continually aware of the batting averages of position players and earned run averages of pitchers throughout major and minor league baseball. If a person had asked me what I wanted to be when I grew up, I would have said, "professional baseball player."

One day, a notice appeared in our daily newspaper announcing a "tryout camp" sponsored by the St. Louis Cardinals, taking place in Battle Creek, Michigan. At the time, I had played only two brief seasons of high school baseball. I was grossly unprepared for such a tryout camp, but the idea of being in close contact with professional baseball coaches for three days absolutely consumed me. I decided to go.

Somehow, I was able to accumulate five dollars. With that amount of money in my pocket, and with my first baseman's glove hooked to my belt, I walked out onto U.S. 131 and headed for Battle Creek. I was sixteen years old.

Hitchhiking along, in and out of one vehicle after another, I eventually came within a few miles of my destination. Finally, a man in a very expensive car picked me up. He asked where I would be staying. I told him I didn't know.

After visiting with me for a few miles, he said, "My wife is away from home for a special event, and you are welcome to stay at my house."

It was an offer too good to turn down. I thanked the gentleman and agreed to stay at his house throughout the tryout camp. Soon, we pulled up in the driveway of a mansion. He then showed me the bedroom I would occupy for the next three days. It was as large as the lower level of our entire Manton house. I had never seen anything like it, and it gave me somewhat of a picture of the way the other part of humanity lives their lives.

The tryout camp more than met my expectations. In spite of my ineptness, the various coaches took time to show me the fundamentals of playing my position. All the St. Louis Cardinals coaches spent camp time teaching individuals how to hit and play their positions. I learned more about baseball fundamentals and techniques during the three-day tryout camp than I did throughout my entire high school baseball career. A problem arose at the termination of the baseball camp, however.

I ran out of money, and I was two hundred miles from home. The subject came up as I chatted with other ballplayers while closing out the camp, and one of the guys offered me a loan of five dollars. I promised to repay as soon as I returned home. Sometimes, however, in spite of best intentions, plans go amiss.

I lost the note with his address, and, in spite of all my efforts, I was simply unable to return his money. Many years later, I was still haunted by the idea of defaulting on a loan.

It was December 8, 1941. As I climbed the steps to the first-floor level of the Manton Junior/Senior High School, I expected to see my eighth-grade classmates carrying on in their usual manner. Normally, boys could be seen "horsing around," good-naturedly pushing and pulling each other around the hallway, while the girls stood off to the side, laughing and keeping an eye on the boys. This particular morning, however, the mood of the students was startlingly subdued. Pulling my friend, Jim Kissinger, aside to a vacant room, I said, "Hey, Jim, what's going on? Is something wrong?"

"Reg, we're at war. Pearl Harbor has been attacked by the Japanese. I thought you would have heard about it over the radio this morning," he reported. It reminded me that unlike most mornings, we had neglected to turn on our radio. There was more to it, however.

Classmate Loretta Jeffers, with perfect attendance from the early grades, was not in school. We soon learned that her brother, Warren, was on the USS *Arizona* battleship at the time of the attack. His family did not know if he had survived the bombing.

For two weeks, the Jeffers family did not know if their son and brother was dead or alive. Finally, a message came through. Warren had been blown off the *Arizona* and had been picked up from the water. Fortunately, he had not been seriously injured.

As I completed my sophomore year at Manton High School, World War II continued to rage. Metal of all kinds was being used to build weaponry and planes, to the point that steel was not available to build cars and farm machinery. Except for a few machinery and auto repair jobs, Ed Sprik and Sons Farm Machinery and Auto Sales was nearly out of business. Brother Harold moved to Detroit to work on war plant construction, while my dad and brother Don alternately drove a truck on war plant construction in Muskegon. Since my dad or my brother was in Muskegon every week, I decided to find out if a Muskegon area war plant might hire a sixteen-year-old. Nearly all able-bodied young men were serving in the military and there was a labor shortage.

After applying at several factories, I finally was hired by the Brunswick Corporation. I was told that I would be working ten hours a day, five days a week and four hours on Saturday. With overtime, I was accumulating a substantial amount of money. Never having learned about money management, however, I later squandered the funds.

Although I had not missed a day of work at the Muskegon factory, a temporary skin problem erupted on my lower body to the point that I was forced to call in sick. Back at the small trailer, our temporary Muskegon residence, I was enjoying listening to my favorite music on our radio when the music suddenly stopped. After a brief pause, a voice came on the air with a major announcement.

Troops from the American, Canadian, and British armies had landed on mainland Europe and an allied invasion had begun. The code word for the day of the landings was "Operation Overlord" or "D-Day." The date was June 6, 1944. Five beachheads were established, and nearly five thousand allied troops were killed, missing, or wounded.

During my early years, our family, like many others, lived on the brink of poverty. Nevertheless, my parents always subscribed to a daily newspaper and one or two weekly newspapers. Since a public library was not accessible, newspapers became my source of reading material. I usually read a significant portion of the entire newspapers, and I read the sports pages from cover to cover and word for word.

One day, I responded to the selection of American League players to the annual All-Star Game as reported by the *Grand Rapids Herald*.

Several mornings later, I opened the newspaper to the sports pages and was absolutely stunned and euphoric to see my letter on the very front of the *Herald* sports pages...

June 19, 1943
SPORT CHATTER
By Heinie Martin
A MANTON, MICH., fan writes in to voice his objection to Pinky Higgins of the Tigers being left off the All-Star team this year.
His letter follows:
"Dear Heinie:

In looking over this year's American league All-Star roster, I noticed the absence of the name of Pinky Higgins. In my mind it surely should be there. Higgins is given little credit for the success of the Tigers. He has always been my favorite ball player and always will be chiefly because he can hit in the clutch. A lot of ball games have been broken up in the late innings by Higgins' ability to come through.

As for his fielding, he comes up with some of the prettiest plays a person ever sees. Maybe some day when a few more people realize the importance of Pinky Higgins at the hot corner and the selecting of the All-Star team is turned over to the fans, as it should be, Higgins will be at the place where he deserves to be – third-base on the All-Star team.

Would you please give me a little history on Pinky Higgins and how he hit the big leagues.

Reggie Sprik,
A Tiger fan from Manton, Mich."

Higgins' Career

PINKY HIGGINS ALSO happens to be one of our favorite ball players. He is one of the best liked men in baseball because he's always a gentleman, on or off the ball field. He's quiet, modest, and retiring and never goes in for those "popoff" roles.

He was born Michael Franklin Higgins and while he's known to the fans as Pinky, his teammates always call him Mike. He was born on May 27, 1909, at Red Oak, Tex., so is now 34 years old. He is Irish, and hunting, golf and bridge are his hobbies.

Pinky is a graduate of the University of Texas, where he played football and baseball. He is the holder of the world's record for consecutive base hits in major league baseball. In June of 1938 he made 12 hits in a row, breaking the record at Briggs stadium while a member of the Boston Red Sox.

Twice Pinky has hit three home runs in one game, and he also holds the record for the most number of chances in a world series game. In the world series of 1940 he handled 10 chances at third base in one game.

Signed Off Campus

HIGGINS WAS SIGNED right off the University of Texas campus. He was signed by Connie Mack and played 14 games in 1930, hitting .250 and fielding 1.000.

He spent the 1931 season at Dallas and San Antonio in the Texas league, where he hit .284. In 1932 he played with Portland in the Pacific Coast league where he batted .325, hitting 33 home runs, 5 triples and 51 doubles, besides driving in 132 runs. That was his greatest season in baseball.

THAT PERFORMANCE brought him back to Philadelphia where he became the regular third baseman in 1933, batting .314 his first full year. The following year he hit .330 and in 1935 he hit .296, clouting 23 home runs and 32 doubles.

In 1936 he batted .289 and at the close of the season was traded to the Boston Red Sox for Bill Werber, also a third baseman. In 1937 he hit .302 for the Red Sox, driving in 106 runs. In 1938 he hit .303 and drove in 106 runs. Rather strangely, he batted almost the identical figure in two successive years and drove in 106 runs each year. To top it off, he hit 5 triples each year.

Throughout my high school career, church services and catechism classes were mandatory, as they had been my entire life. Our rural church was small in membership and located in a rather remote location. Sermons were excruciatingly long and boring.

Wednesday evening catechism classes were a different matter, however. Classes began at seven o'clock and lasted an hour. Since my parents regularly loaned me the family car for such a purpose, I was able to prearrange for a later evening date with a lovely lady. Again, some trade-offs are really worthwhile.

Most of the boys in my high school, particularly athletes, had steady girlfriends. But that was not my romantic style. I preferred being what might be called a "dater." Prior to a school social event, or if a good movie was showing in Cadillac, I might simply ask a nice looking girl for a date. I avoided interfering with romances of other athletes. On the next occasion, I might request a date with a different girl. Consequently, I seldom felt socially restricted.

"Well, you have to make a decision; you can't play two different instruments in one band." It was Mr. Jim Read, our junior high and high school band director. I had begun my eighth-grade year in a Manton Rural Agricultural School, having completed my kindergarten through seventh-grade studies at the Arlene Country School. To my utter dismay, even though I was only in eighth grade, Mr. Read had asked me to join the high school band with my hand-me-down clarinet. It was obvious that he wanted to add bodies to, and help fill out, the marching band. "I can't play a note," I told Mr. Read. "Just move your fingers around and pretend," I was told. So, the band director traded in my integrity for what he considered the overall good of the band. I was uncomfortable with the idea, but marched along, like a robot.

In the meantime, I was playing trombone in the junior high band. That is what prompted Mr. Read's statement about playing two different instruments.

But, I had heard my oldest brother, Harold, play a beautiful trombone solo in church, and I had also listened on a vinyl record to the inimitable Artie Shaw front his big band playing "Begin the Beguine" on his clarinet. But now I was compelled to make a perplexing decision. Since I aspired to play dance band music in the future, I believed the clarinet to be the best choice. The trombone would have to wait.

As I moved along through high school band, I worked my way up to second chair, but never reached first chair status. That was because my cousin, Ray Aten, occupied the first clarinet chair, and he was better at reading the black dots on the band music. After running through our clarinet part a few times, however, I simply played by ear. At any rate, if our music was blown off our music stands, my cousin would need to scramble to get it back together, while I could simply keep on playing.

Although some band members considered band practice to be boring, I did not feel that way. To me, band practice and physical education classes were the highlights of the school day.

Many years later, as Marilyn and I stepped from our vehicle and walked down the sidewalk toward an open-air dance pavilion, the magic of Glenn Miller's arrangement of "Moonlight Serenade" permeated the atmosphere. I was overcome by emotion as I mentally traveled back in time to the glory days of the big bands. I didn't believe it would ever happen in my lifetime, but here it was being played in a Traverse City open-air dance pavilion by a swing band. I was euphoric.

It was a most memorable trip back in time to high school and college days when the big band sounds of Guy Lombardo, Les Brown, and the Dorsey Brothers took over the numerous ballrooms, hotel dance floors, and national radio waves throughout the nation.

Actually, Benny Goodman, Glenn Miller, and numerous other famous bandleaders got their start in the 1930s and some even began in the 1920s. So, by the time I arrived in high school in 1942, big band sounds were the music of the day. During noon hours, we danced in the school gym to 78-rpm records that provided songs like Glenn Miller's "In the Mood," "Tuxedo Junction," and "A String of Pearls." Also popular at the time were Tommy Dorsey's "I'm Getting Sentimental Over You" and Artie Shaw's "Begin the Beguine." I was fascinated with the big band style of music. So, it was not a surprise that a group of us came together to try to emulate it.

It was early in my junior year in high school when we began to meet in various homes to put it all together. Either Delores Johnson or Patty Lommen was on piano, Bud Kleckler on woodwind, Mel Carpenter on vocals, Dan Cook on the drum set, and I was on clarinet. We must have liked the color blue, as two of our numbers that I best remember are "Blue Skies" and "My Blue Heaven."

Sports, Music, and ... War

In that era, each class earned its own money for a senior trip. Each class selected its own treasurer, who was responsible for the class funds collected and spent. To say these class treasurers were frugal would be an understatement. "Tightfisted" would be a more appropriate description. They all seemed to fear coming up short of money for their senior trip planned for their class.

Consequently, our band played most of the school dances. Not because we were the best band in the area, but because, with various class treasurers' approval, we could be hired for a very low price.

As a student in the Arlene Country School, I was not very well liked by the five other people in my class. I knew that because whenever classmates had an opportunity to vote for a person to fill a role of any kind, I would be the last person chosen. I was not a favorite of any of my Arlene schoolteachers, either, as is reflected by my elementary report cards. That's why I was shocked when I was elected president of my ninth-grade class in Manton High School.

In tenth grade, I was not elected to a class office. The student body, however, elected me to the presidency of the student council. After being elected eleventh-grade class president, I learned that I would be performing a special role.

Traditionally, the junior class president served as toastmaster at the Junior/Senior Banquet, which immediately preceded the Senior Prom. This would be a major school event. Faculty, as well as upper class students, were expected to attend. I would need to prepare. I gathered a few bits of humor to introduce the various speakers and musicians, but Mr. Crisp, our commercial teacher and guest speaker, "turned the tables" on me.

"Reggie," he said, "was out on a date with his girlfriend. They decided to talk about 'kith and kin.' So, Reggie asked, 'kin I kith you?', and his girlfriend replied, 'yeth, you kin.'" The audience roared, and I didn't realize my face could turn so red.

It was the summer of 1945. Bob Cunningham and I, along with two other baseball players, decided to attend a few Detroit Tigers baseball games. Bob had relatives in Detroit, which would give us a place to sleep. After two games, the car owner and one other ballplayer returned to Manton. Bob and I would hitchhike.

At seven o'clock in the evening on August 15 of that 1945 summer, Bob Cunningham and I stood beside a string of streetcars in downtown Detroit. Suddenly, and with no warning, everything around us erupted.

"The war is over! The war is over!!" people shouted at the top of their lungs. President Truman had just made the announcement. Rods connecting streetcars to power sources were disconnected. People with brown bags pulled out wine and whiskey bottles, which were passed in and out through now opened streetcar windows. Bob and I both took a gulp from a whiskey bottle.

The place was a screaming madhouse. Fathers, brothers, sisters, sons, and daughters would soon return home from Pacific Island death traps and from ships and submarines in torpedo-infested waters. Some had already experienced the return of their loved one with arms or legs blown off, or, worse, in a body bag. Family after family had lived in continual fear of the arrival of a telegram notifying them of the death of their family member. Four hundred and twenty thousand United States soldiers, sailors, Marines, and Air Force members gave their lives for their nation.

In total, throughout the world, sixty million people were killed. All of this was because of one man—German Nazi leader Adolf Hitler.

The office of the school superintendent was glassed in and overlooked the high school main hallway, through which students moved from one classroom to another. One morning, Superintendent Bennett announced a high school assembly to take place immediately after lunch.

"I've noticed," stated Mr. Bennett, "that quite a few of our students are becoming careless about their personal grooming. So, I'm going to have a full-length mirror installed in the hallway so that you see for yourself as to whether or not you are properly groomed." Mr. Bennett then went on to explain the importance of self-image before dismissing us to our regular classes. A few days later, a full-length mirror did, indeed, appear at the end of our hallway.

Along with administrative duties, Mr. Bennett always taught one class each semester or full school year. One day, near the end of my freshman year, he stopped me in the hallway.

"Reginald," he always called me Reginald, "I will be teaching geometry next year, and I want you in my class." I hated math, and the thought of being in a geometry class made me want to flee.

I had, so far, dodged algebra by choosing the option of a class called junior business training. "I can't take geometry," I explained to Mr. Bennett, "I haven't taken algebra." I was under the assumption that algebra was a requirement prior to studying geometry.

"Oh, that's all right, Reginald, you'll do fine in my geometry class. I'll be expecting you." I was doomed.

Mr. Bennett turned out to be one of the best teachers of my high school days. He was full of enthusiasm, and he made classes exceptionally interesting. Later, when I built our house from the ground up, I was able to use much of the information I had acquired from Mr. Bennett's geometry class.

One year after that geometry class, I accidently met Mr. Bennett in the hallway. "Mr. Bennett," I said, "I'd like to go to college. What do you think about that?"

"Well, Reginald," Mr. Bennett replied, "I really don't think you are college material."

During those glorious high school days, a phenomenon occurred that has impacted the Manton school, the students and faculty, and the entire community to this very day.

Earlier, while living in Arlene, someone in a leadership position in that small community arranged for a federal grant to build a small gym to be attached to the country school that my cousin Ray Aten and I attended. Although the gym was unheated, there was usually a basketball available and Ray and I spent considerable time shooting baskets. Although we didn't become proficient, we did learn how to dribble and handle a basketball. To this day, I am not aware of any other country school with a gym attached.

At the same time, a group of talented athletes was moving through the grades in the Manton school system. By the time we had reached tenth grade, four of us in that group were promoted to the varsity basketball team, and three of us were starters. At first we struggled somewhat, but as the season moved along, the team began to jell and by tournament time we were in high gear. We took the district championship and went through to the regional finals, rather overwhelmingly defeating teams that had beaten us earlier in the year.

At the beginning of the basketball season in the eleventh grade, Ray Aten, who had lived in Grand Rapids the previous year, returned to our basketball program measuring six-foot five-inches tall. Meanwhile Bob Cunningham and I had reached six-foot plus in height. At this point, our starting lineup was comprised of Dan Cook, a gifted outside shooter, Dutch Dontje, a terrific ball handler and defensive specialist, Ray Aten at center, and Bob Cunningham and I at the forward positions. We were all juniors and as the basketball season got underway, the magic began to happen.

Carrying over the momentum of the previous season's tournament run, we hit the ground running, so to speak. We rung up one victory after another, losing only one game for the entire season. That loss was reversed later in the season when we played that team a second time. We entered the district tournament full of confidence and expecting to make a strong tournament run, perhaps all the way to the state finals. But, alas, it was not to be.

Perhaps we were overconfident. There were also unconfirmed rumors that two starters had been partying the previous night. Whatever the reason, we proceeded to lose the district championship game to a team that wasn't really very good. A team that, in fact, lost their next tournament game. I have memories of our shots bouncing off rims and air balls fired skyward by our outside shooters—we seemed to be completely out of rhythm the entire game. The Manton community was extremely disappointed after our 16-win season, our coach was devastated, and as players, we were stunned. It made us realize the vulnerability of a basketball team, regardless of their won-loss record.

The period of time of our senior year was, indeed, a wonderful, feel-good time for everyone. Germany and Japan had been defeated. Brothers, fathers, sons, and daughters were safely returning home from serving in World War II. Homes were being built, new cars were being bought, softball leagues were forming under newly lighted fields. It seemed that the world was everyone's oyster. In the midst of all this was a small-town basketball team comprised of five starting seniors with very capable reserves. Reserves were made up of two seniors, two juniors, and one sophomore. The five starters were all returnees from the two-loss team of the past season. Hopes were extremely high for a very strong tournament run, but flashbacks of the previous tournament loss lurked in our memories.

Manton High School 1945/1946 Basketball Season

Date	Manton Score	Opponent & Score	Where
Nov. 30	37	Mesick 4	Mesick
Dec. 7	43	McBain 19	McBain
Dec. 11	19	Houghton Lake 11	Manton
Dec. 14	37	Cadillac 20	Cadillac
Dec. 18	34	Benzonia 9	Manton
Dec. 21	48	Frankfort 36	Frankfort
Jan. 11	53	Lake City 23	Lake City
Jan. 18	47	Northport 30	Manton
Jan. 25	41	Big Rapids 25	Big Rap-ids
Feb. 1	52	Frankfort 22	Manton
Feb. 5	41	Kalkaska 13	Kalkaska
Feb. 8	44	Big Rapids 31	Manton
Feb. 15	49	Mesick 18	Manton
Feb. 19	54	McBain 23	Manton
Feb. 22	48	Cadillac 36	Manton
Mar. 1	56	Lake City 25	Manton

In order to get us accustomed to tough competition, two Class B schools, Big Rapids and Cadillac, were added to the schedule.

Manton Defeated Big Rapids There Friday 41 to 25
Playing at Big Rapids last Friday night Manton met what it is believed will be the toughest opposition during the regular schedule, and defeated Big Rapids by a score of 41 to 25. Sprik was high for Manton with 16 points. It was a triumph for a smooth working Class C team over a strong Class B outfit. Manton Reserves also took their game 22 to 20.

In the nine games played to date, Manton Rangers have earned a total of 359 points, compared to 178 points scored by their opponents.

A lot of emphasis was placed on defense. Basically, we simply rolled over every team we played. In one game, for example, our opponent did not make one single field goal the entire game. Their only points came on free throws, and their total points for the game amounted to single digits.

Manton & Lake City In Finals Tonight

The Manton and Lake City high school basketball teams will meet in the Class C district finals at Manton tonight at 9:15 and Houghton Lake and Merritt meet in the Class D finals at 7:30.

Lake City earned the right to meet Manton by defeating McBain last night by a 50 to 27 count. Mason was high scorer for Lake City with 20 points and Bogard was high for McBain with 6 points.

Manton defeated Marion 43 to 27 to go into the finals and while Manton won by a 16-point margin Marion was in there fighting all the way and were only behind 23 to 16 at half time and were behind 28 to 21 at three quarter time. Ray Aten of Manton with 16 points was high point man and his teammate Sprik was a close second with 14 points. Riber was high for Marion with 7.

District Title is Won by Manton H.S.

Manton and Houghton Lake were crowned the district basketball champions Saturday night at Manton.

Manton, the Class C champions, had a hard time of it and it wasn't until the final whistle blew that they emerged victors over Lake City by a 3-point margin of 38 to 35.

Lake City took a 10 to 6 lead at quarter time. At halftime the game was all even at 18 each. At the three-quarter mark Manton trailed 30 to 27 and in the final period racked up 11 points to 5 for Lake City.

Sprik of Manton and Mason of Lake City were high point honors with 18 each.

Houghton Lake had an easy time of it winning the Class D championship, beating Merritt by a 47 to 28 count. Cornell of Houghton Lake was high point man with 21. Mead was high for Merritt with 12.

Fortunately, our team entered the state tournaments 100-percent healthy and injury-free. Furthermore, Coach Lyon made a defensive change which significantly affected our total offense and my scoring role on the team. We mainly played a zone defense, and I was moved from the front court to the back court because of my rebounding ability. Prior to that pre-tournament move, I had spent my previous two years in the front court on defense. Because I had sprinter speed, I scored many points on steals and fast breaks down the floor. So, overall, we improved on rebounding but definitely lost an edge as to fast break baskets, as neither front court players had my down-court speed. I also had picked up rebound shots off our fast break. There is no doubt, however, it was a wise move by Coach Lyon.

Manton Meets Clare on Road to State Cage Championship

Manton's Rangers studied the strategy of the Clare quintet today, their next obstacle on the road to the state Class C championship. The Rangers pounded out a determined 36 to 32 victory over Charlevoix Saturday night at Petoskey to sweep through regional competition.

It was the first time since 1920 that Manton has emerged victorious from regional play. In 1941 the Wexford County team was eliminated by Harbor Springs, 11 to 31, and again in 1944 the north enders made it through the district tourney, only to lose to Pellston, 34-12.

Undefeated in the 1945-46 season, the Rangers stretched a one-point lead over Charlevoix in the first quarter to seven points at the half; nine at the three-quarter mark, and then nipped an opposition rally to hold a four-point lead at the final gun.

The Rangers will play Clare in the State quarter-finals Thursday night at Midland. The game is at 7 p.m.

Aten once again took scoring honors in the Charlevoix game. The star center of the Manton offensive combination scored 17 points while teammates Cook, Sprik and Cunningham scored 7, 6 and 6, respectively.

The first string five played throughout the game.

R. Carey of Charlevoix sparked his team's efforts with 12 points.

The Midland tourney will attract a number of northern counties' fans as Traverse City, winner of the Petoskey regional in Class B competition, also plays there Thursday night. The Traverse City – Alma game is scheduled for 8:30 p.m.

Winners of the Manton-Clare battle will play the winners of the Whitehall-Kalamazoo (St. Augustine) tilt on March 22nd at the Michigan State College Fieldhouse, Lansing.

SPORT In the News!
Friday, March 22, 1946   **Cadillac, (Mich.) Evening News**

Manton Defeats Clare
Play St. Augustine of Kalamazoo in Semi-Finals Game

Manton's Rangers, after breezing through their encounter with the highly regarded Clare quintet 47 to 34 at Midland last night, rested in their Lansing hotel rooms today ready for the semi-finals clash with St. Augustine of Kalamazoo.

The north county team, making Manton history with their trip to the finals, took a three-point lead over Clare in the first quarter and steadily increased it until the final quarter when the reserves were put in.

Cunningham of Manton was high point man with 14 tallies. Aten came out second-best on the scoring honors with 13 points.

An estimated 300 Manton high school students and team fans accompanied the team to Midland. It was the first time in the history of state competition that the Rangers were able to survive district and regional play. In 1941 and again in 1944 the Wexford county team went into the regionals, but each time were defeated in their first games.

Coach Dick Lyon put his second string into play during the last three minutes of the game.

The Rangers will play St. Augustine of Kalamazoo on the Michigan State Fieldhouse gymnasium floor at 10 p.m. tonight in the semi-finals. St. Augustine defeated Whitehall 34 to 27 last night.

Box Score
MANTON

Player	FG	FT	TP
Sprik	4	3	11
Cunningham	6	2	14
Aten	5	3	13
H. Dontje	0	0	0

Box Score (continued)
MANTON

Player	FG	FT	TP
Cook	3	3	9
G. Dontje	0	0	0
W. Lutke	0	0	0
Larson	0	0	0
Allen	0	0	0
Totals	**18**	**11**	**47**

CLARE

Player	FG	FT	TP
Perry	0	0	0
Koslin	3	0	6
Cappaert	2	1	5
Kane	1	0	2
Rodebaugh	4	3	11
Newman	3	0	6
Smith	1	2	4
Totals	**14**	**6**	**34**

Following our victory over Charlevoix in the regional finals, we defeated Clare in the quarterfinals. We then went on to overcome Kalamazoo St. Augustine (renamed Kalamazoo Hackett) in the semifinals.

Box Score:
MANTON

Player	FG	FT	TP
Cunningham	0	0	0
Sprik	3	8	14
Aten	9	3	21
H. Dontje	0	0	0
Cook	3	2	8
G. Dontje	0	1	1
Totals	**15**	**14**	**44**

ST. AUGUSTINE

Lacala	3	4	10
Moreland	1	0	2
Pocernik	4	1	9
Walker	2	0	4
Menzie	1	1	3
Scott	2	0	4
Totals	**13**	**6**	**32**

Manton – 44; Kalamazoo – 32

The Manton boys played hard and brilliant basketball Friday night in defeating the Kalamazoo St. Augustines to keep in the championship running. The Rangers were never in trouble in this game, and had a substantial lead at the end of each period.

Aten was high with 21 points, Reg Sprik had 14 and Cook 8. Manton led at the first period 9 to 5, at the half 22 to 15, third-quarter 35 to 25 and maintained this ratio to win the contest 44 to 32.

CADILLAC EVENING NEWS
Wexford – Cadillac – Missaukee's Home Daily, Michigan
Saturday, March 23, 1946

MANTON WINS AGAIN
Defeats St. Augustine in Semi-Finals Clash, 44-32

The Manton Rangers set their sights on the state class "C" trophy today, following their decisive 12-point defeat of Kalamazoo St. Augustine, 44 to 32.

The north enders come up against their toughest competition of the thrill-packed tournament tonight. They will meet Saginaw St. Peter and Paul in the finals at the Jenison Fieldhouse, East Lansing. The Saginaw five run tall and rangy, the team average topping even the Rangers who are sparked by the six-foot four-inch Aten. Saginaw won their game last night with Jackson St. Mary's 46 to 27.

Manton has gone basketball mad while watching its team maintain a sensational undefeated, untied record through game after game of the conference season. Not since the Charlevoix contest in the regionals has the Rangers supremacy been seriously challenged. More than 200 students and fans made the trip to Midland and followed the team to East Lansing as they romped through the quarter finals and semi-final rounds.

Aten again set the pace for scoring in last night's game, piling up 21 of the teams 44 points. Sprik was second, with 14. Lacala of Kalamazoo led the opponents with 10 tallies.

The game featured Manton's use of its rangy center to garner points, while St. Augustine favored the small but speedy Lacala for a fast attack.

St. Augustine caused a wave of dismay in the Manton cheering section during the first two minutes of play when they grabbed the lead. By the end of the first quarter, however, the Wexford youths had regained command, 9 to 5. Stretched to 22-15 at the half the northerners coasted along to 35-25 at the three-quarter mark and finished with 44 to 32.

The game was marked by a large number of fouls. St. Augustine was charged with 23 and the Rangers with 10.

Our state championship game was against Saginaw Sts. Peter and Paul (now a part of Saginaw Nouvel, following a consolidation). Each team was undefeated, so a showdown of showdowns was anticipated. We did not disappoint. With seconds left on the clock, Manton was ahead by one point and was in possession of the ball. But a Saginaw player stole the ball and headed for the basket. Dan Cook finally caught up to him and fouled him as he shot, causing the ball to go astray.

Jenison Fieldhouse, with eleven thousand people, its largest crowd ever for a state tournament game, was a screaming madhouse as the two teams were either tied or nearly so through the entire game and now it came down to this. As the game came down to the wire, one avid Manton fan went under the stands, unable to deal with the pressure of the situation.

So, with two seconds left on the clock, and our team up by one point, a Saginaw player went to the free throw line for two free throws. Sinking one shot would put the game into overtime. Two shots through the net would have given Saginaw the victory.

The first free throw bounced off the front of the rim, assuring us at least a tie and overtime. Six-foot-five Ray Aten was on one side of the lane next to the basket and I was on the other side. The ball hit the

Sports, Music, and ... War

back of the rim, bounced once, and came off on Ray's side. He went up, grabbed the ball, held it for two seconds and the Michigan Class C State Championship was ours.

CADILLAC, (MICH.) EVENING NEWS
Manton Rangers Capture State Class "C" Crown
Win Over Saginaw, 34-33, In Thrill-Packed Contest

Manton's Rangers climaxed a phenomenal season Saturday night with a victory over Saginaw Sts. Peter and Paul parochial school, 34 to 33 in the last minute of play, to win the state class "C" title.

A rabbit foot in the pocket of someone of the more than 200 hysterical Manton fans must have figured prominently in winning the game as a hushed crowd watched Leo Beeg of Saginaw miss two free throws in the last five seconds of play – free throws that could have either won or tied the game.

Easily the most spectacular game of the state tourney, the Manton-Saginaw battle had the 11,000 cage fans in and out of their seats throughout the game. The Rangers were able to maintain a small lead through the first three quarters of the game, but things looked black for the north enders when Saginaw put on a spurt with four minutes left to play and tied the score at 30-all. Another bucket put Saginaw ahead by two points, as Andy Strongrich, diminutive guard, found the range on long shots.

With two minutes left to play, Manton knotted the score again. Saginaw sank a free throw for a one-point lead which was reversed with a field goal from the corner by Bob Cunningham, dependable Ranger guard.

Then came the stinger. Leo Beeg was fouled under the basket in the final, desperate melee of the last five seconds. Under strain that would have rattled a professional Beeg made his two tries for extra points. Both connected too solidly with the hoop and rolled out.

Both teams took an undefeated record into the final battle for state honors.

The score was tied five times during the game, yet at the end of each quarter Manton was ahead. The first quarter ended 13-7; the second 20-19; the third 23-22 and the final with the historic 34-33.

It was Manton's 23rd successive victory.

In other finals contests Holland defeated Saginaw Arthur Hill 43 to 40 in class A; St. Joseph took an easy 33 to 26 game from Fenton in class B, and Bridgman ran its record of consecutive wins to 41 with a 42 to 27 win over Detroit Country Day. Bridgman was class D winner in 1945.

Box Score:

MANTON

Player	FG	FT	TP
Sprik, forward	2	0	4
Cunningham, forward	2	0	4
Aten, center	3	3	9
Cook, guard	5	4	14
H. Dontje, guard	1	1	3
G. Dontje, guard	0	0	0
Totals	**13**	**8**	**34**

SAGINAW SS. PETER AND PAUL

Player	FG	FT	TP
Rushlow, forward	3	2	8
Beeg, forward	1	1	3
Kruske, forward	0	0	0
McColgan, center	5	1	11
Lunning, guard	2	0	4
Strongrich, guard	3	1	7
Kwaiser, guard	0	0	0
Kelsa, guard	0	0	0
Totals	**14**	**5**	**33**

Manton	**13-7-3-11**	**34**
Saginaw P&P	**7-12-3-11**	**33**

Tournaments Leading to the Championship

	Manton Score	Opponent & Score
District	43	Marion 27
District	38	Lake City 35
Regional	35	Traverse City St. Francis 23
Regional	36	Charlevoix 32
Quarter Final	47	Clare 34
Semi Final	44	Kalamazoo St. Augustine 32
FINAL	34	Saginaw SS Peter and Paul 33

Over the course of our last two seasons, and with the same starting five throughout, we had won a total of forty-one games with only two losses.

Coming home from Lansing the next day, we found business places throughout the community decorated with orange and black. A downtown dance was held in our honor with prominent local musicians donating their time and talent. We were on stage to loud applause from a large crowd at the Lyric Theatre in Cadillac. A dinner was held in our honor. On and on it went and orange and black seemed to be everywhere.

Back row, l to r: Coach Dick Lyon, Larry Williams, Don Larson, Manager Leslie Gibbs, Al Lutke, Grover Dontje, Superintendent of Schools Jim Read.
Front row, l to r: Dan Cook, Reggie Sprik, Ray Aten, Bob Cunningham, Harold (Dutch) Dontje, Jerry Allen.

Team members were Jerry Allen, Ray Aten, Dan Cook, Bob Cunningham, Grover Dontje, Harold "Dutch" Dontje, Don Larson, Al Lutke, Larry Williams, and Reg Sprik. Dick Lyon was the coach.

During its tournament run, Manton defeated, in order, Marion, Lake City, Traverse City St. Francis, Charlevoix, Clare, Kalamazoo St. Augustine, and, finally, Saginaw Sts. Peter and Paul.

On the road to the 1946 State Class C Basketball Championship, the Manton team won twenty-three consecutive games. Included were two regular season wins over Big Rapids and two victories over Cadillac.

The Saginaw team entered the finals undefeated, with a record of twenty-four consecutive wins. Game action was furious, and the lead changed hands five times before Manton emerged victoriously. Many years later, the Michigan High School Athletic Association classified the Saginaw-Manton game as the most exciting game in state tournament history.

The Tribune-Record
Manton, Michigan
Friday, March 29, 1946
Rangers Win Thriller to Take State Championship
Cool, Hard and Clean Playing Brings Manton State Championship for First Time

This basketball-minded community is returning to normalcy again after a week of tense excitement which culminated at East Lansing Saturday night when the Manton Rangers became the State Class C champions by their defeat of St. Peter and St. Paul of Saginaw, 34 to 33. Thus, the State Championship came to Manton for the first time.

Ever since Manton won the district championship here two weeks ago the community has been traveling, first to Petoskey for the game with Traverse City St. Francis and the crucial regional championship game which the Rangers won from Charlevoix, then to Midland when Manton cooled the enthusiastic Clare boys who were regional champs at Mt. Pleasant. The wild enthusiasm of this community in their winning team offset any distance handicap, and Manton turned up in large numbers at East Lansing for the final games. Anxious stay-at-homes kept the telephones hot at game-end time for word of the contests.

It was a large crowd of Manton boosters who saw the Rangers defeat the Saginaw parochials in the finals Saturday night by a slim one-point margin. Not only was this community there in numbers, but many former residents made the trip to see this championship struggle.

As for the game, it was a thriller from start to finish. Although the Rangers led at the end of every period, they were behind several times in the game by one point. The score was tied five times. Only in the first quarter did Manton have a commanding lead, the score at the end of this period standing at 13 to 7. After that it was a tough see-saw battle. Score at the half was 20 to 19; at the third-quarter 23 to 22.

Winning Basket

As time was running out and with Manton behind one point, Bob Cunningham looped in what turned out to be the winning field basket in the last 45 seconds of play. The game might have gone to Saginaw in the last seconds of play, but for failure of Leo Beeg of Saginaw to connect with two free throws. An instant after his second throw missed, the gun ended the game.

All of the Manton boys played a fine game. Danny Cook stood out as a star, collecting 14 points for individual honors. Cook tossed in three long-shot field goals, besides his free throws.

MANTON

Players	FG	FT	TP
Sprik, forward	2	0	4
Cunningham, forward	2	0	4
Aten, center	3	3	9
Cook, guard	5	4	14
H. Dontje, guard	1	1	3
G. Dontje, guard	0	0	0
Totals	**13**	**3**	**34**

SAGINAW SS. PETER AND PAUL

Players	FG	FT	TP
Lushlow, forward	3	2	8
Beeg, forward	1	1	3
Kruske, forward	0	0	0
McColgan, center 5	1	11	
Lunning, guard	2	0	4
Strongrich, guard 3	1	7	
Kwaiser, guard	0	0	0
Kelso, guard	0	0	0
Totals	**14**	**5**	**33**

Manton to Honor Winning Cage Team

A "Spring Frolic," honoring the Manton basketball team, state champions, and their coach, Richard Lyon, will be given in the Odd Fellows Hall, Manton, Friday evening from 8 to 12.

The Party is being sponsored by the Odd Fellows, Rebekahs, and the school faculty and is open to all the young people of the community.

Music will be furnished by the Manton Rhythm Makers. The grand march will start at nine o'clock and a floor show will be at 9:30. The hall will be decorated for the occasion and there will be favors for all.

Crowd Sets
New Record
At Tourney
Manton, Bridgman, St. Joseph
Also Champions Before 10,971 Persons
By GEORGE S. ADERTON
(State Journal Sports Editor)

Largest crowd ever to attend an indoor athletic event at Michigan State college, 10,971 persons, saw four basketball champions crowned in jam-packed Jenison Fieldhouse at Michigan State college last night as high school teams contested for titles in the finals of the lower peninsula tournament. Every ticket printed for the event was sold.

A crown that ebbed and flowed, and came and went, as the colorful pageant of schoolboy sports unfolded, packed every corner of the Spartans' huge sports palace. The contests, spiritedly played, had the throng in an uproar for more than five consecutive hours.

The Champions:
Class A – Holland
Class B – St. Joseph
Class C – Manton
Class D – Bridgman

Rangers Win Thriller to Take State Championship Sidelights

– The entire community joins this paper in congratulating our State Champions. What a team! And don't forget, too, the able coaching of Dick Lyon.

– One ardent Manton fan just couldn't take it, and when Saginaw was given two free shots in the final seconds of Saturday's game, he got up,

Display in the lobby of the Manton High School gymnasium.

turned his back on the game and started out. Two seconds later the gun went off and he had to ask someone how the game came out.

– Ray Aten, Manton's star center, was hurt by a blow on the back of his head which sent him sprawling to the floor and temporarily dazed. He continued in the game after time was called. Sprik was out for a short time from nosebleed.

– We hear that a former coach Elmer Rewalt of Allegan, and the Don Nelsons of Durand, former teachers here, were at the game.

– Supt. James Read was ill with the flu all the time he was in Lansing. He got out of bed just long enough to see the games.

– Some of the Manton fans really can take it. They drove down for the games both days, spending most of both nights driving home.

– Pictures of the team were printed in the Grand Rapids Herald Sunday, and the Grand Rapids Press Monday. Detroit and Lansing papers gave the final game a good play. This is quite a contrast to rather poor publicity at Petoskey when Manton won from Charlevoix.

– The beautiful trophies won by the Rangers this year are on display in the Earl Williams market window. These include the district, regional and State trophies, and also the Northwestern Michigan conference trophy.

– That Manton's victory was a brilliant one can be seen by the fact that there are some 200 Class C basketball teams in the state.

Donald Nelsons
Praise Champions

Bob Cunningham and other members of the basketball team have received this letter from Donald and Elaine Nelson, of Durand, former teachers here:

Dear Bob (and the Manton Rangers): Elaine and I just got home from East Lansing where we witnessed one of the most thrilling and most pleasurable events during our five years in Michigan – the crowning of the Manton Rangers as the Class C Champions of Lower Michigan. May we extend our sincere and heartiest congratulations to all of you and your fine coach. We sat as tense and as breathless in those closing moments of the game as any Manton fan and our hearts were with all of you, many of whom were former pupils and friends.

I wish you would convey to Dick Lyon and to each of the boys on the squad our hearty congratulations. Tell them that we are proud of them and their splendid record and that we are inclined to boast to our friends down here in Durand that we once taught in Manton and had some of these same boys in our classes there.

LATER NEWSPAPER ARTICLE
MANTON CLASS C STATE CHAMPIONS, 1946

When Richard Lyon came to Manton in the early 1940's he was used to winning basketball games. Before coming to Manton, the teams he coached at Bellaire High School won three districts and one regional championship. With the same enthusiasm and skill that worked at Bellaire, Lyon came to Manton and compiled an impressive 65-11 record from 1943-1946 when his team won the state championship.

Basketball playing rules were different in the days following World War II. The three-second rule did not exist, and this allowed players to take more time to set up plays and for shooting. Most players shot two handed.

A huge following of avid basketball fans followed the Manton team through the 1945-46 season as they won all 16 regular season games. Manton was a class "C" school, but this did not stop them from playing large schools such as Traverse City, Big Rapids and Cadillac. The Rangers humiliated the larger Big Rapids team so badly on their own court there was a near riot on the floor after the game.

As they entered the District Playoff in March 1946, Manton was not favored to go very far even though they were undefeated. The team was not rated by the newspapers, but this did not deter the loyal Manton fans who believed in their team.

After winning the District Championship, which was held in Manton's tiny gymnasium, (torn down in the early 1960's) the Rangers traveled to Petoskey where they played Traverse City St. Francis in the Regional semi-finals. In the regional finals Manton defeated the highly rated Charlevoix team that many had predicted were state championship caliber.

Fresh from their victories in Northern Michigan, the Rangers journeyed to Midland where they easily defeated Clare 47-34. The following night Manton defeated Kalamazoo St. Augustine 44-32 at Jenison Fieldhouse in East Lansing in the semi-finals.

The citizens of Manton were in a frenzy. Basketball dominated the conversation and thoughts of everyone in the community. Three bus loads of students and car loads of families drove to East Lansing, to watch their hometown boys. One family that drove down to see the semi-finals felt compelled to stay for the finals the following night so they slept in their car that March night as they could not afford a motel.

In the game that has been described as being the most spectacular of the state tournaments Manton was pitted against a very strong, highly rated and undefeated team: Saginaw St. Peter and Paul.

Before the largest crowd ever to attend an indoor athletic event at Michigan State college, Manton and St. Peter and Paul had the people on their feet shouting hysterically throughout the game.

For the first three quarters Manton maintained a small lead but with about four minutes remaining Saginaw tied the score, regained the ball and sunk another basket putting them in the lead. Manton, playing as if their lives were at stake, grabbed the ball with two minutes to play remaining and sunk a shot which tied the game for the fifth time. With time running short for both teams Saginaw was fouled by a Ranger and scored a free throw.

Down by one, 33-32, Manton moved down court in control of the ball. With 45 seconds remaining in the game Bob Cunningham made a lay-up putting Manton ahead by one point: 34-33.

Saginaw moved down court and positioned themselves for one final basket.

With two seconds remaining Saginaw's forward Leo Beeg attempted a shot but was fouled. The tension was unbearable for players and fans alike. One avid Manton fan, unable to stand the pressure got up and left.

In a finish that will never be forgotten both Leo Beeg's shots hit the rim, bounced up and rolled out, which clinched the state championship for Manton.

Coach Richard Lyon and his team returned to Manton in triumph and were treated to a hero's welcome. The towns people were in a state of ecstasy and rightly so.

It was once said that Coach Lyon was the winningest coach Manton ever had. He recognized talent and helped players develop confidence in themselves. He was not excitable and whether his team was winning or losing he was always smiling.

When asked why he allowed one of his players to shoot in such an unorthodox manner he answered, "I don't care how the ball goes through the hoop as long as it comes out the bottom." Such was his philosophy and who can dispute it worked.

THE MANTON SUN – Manton, Michigan
Monday, March 31, 1975 – Page 10
Manton School News

NOBODY LEFT IN TOWN!

I believe it was Jud Arnett who wrote recently in the Detroit Free Press about his experience as a reporter in Ohio, when a little community named Farmer Center won a state basketball championship in the forties. He mentioned this after commenting about White Cloud here in Michigan, this year, and the enthusiasm of the whole community. Well, I just thought I would like to make a few comments about the City of Manton in the school year of 1945-46, when the Rangers took it all. Basketball was really big that year. Especially to those of us in the community that knew boys such as Ray Aten; Bob Cunningham; Reg Sprik; Danny Cook; Harold Dontje; Jerry Allen; Larry Williams; Donald Larson, Alvin Lutke; and Grover Dontje. Naturally, some played more than others, but we didn't have just a good team, we had a great one, and the closer they got to the finals, the more the excitement grew, until Manton won the Class "C" basketball championship in a real cliff hanger by a score of 34 to 33. Your retiring school superintendent was then teaching full time, and saying, "Well, if they win this one, I'll go to just one more." When that last game was over, I could scarcely speak, and Paul Prothero asked me from under the stands (he couldn't stand the agony of those last two free throws, when Saginaw St. Peter and Paul sent Leo Beeg to the line) "Who won?" Had Beeg made one of those free throws in that last two seconds, there would have been *an overtime, no doubt. And had he made both of them, Saginaw would have been the state champs. I'll always remember how coach Richard E. Lyon was the perfect gentleman through it all. Fans screaming so loud that when I kept the home score book, I couldn't hear the other scorer right next to me even though he yelled at the top of his voice. Yes, some of us really know what White Cloud and Farmer Center, Ohio, went through. There indeed is no substitute for VICTORY, no matter how you slice it. As I said, in 1946, when the Rangers hit the road, there wasn't anyone left in town.*

Throughout the regular season and tournament run, the Manton team received tremendous support from students, faculty, parents, and fans. Finally, this quote from the March 29, 1946, edition of the *Manton Tribune Record*, "The entire community joins this newspaper in congratulating our State Champions. **What a team!**"

Army days. Served from October 1, 1946, until March 28, 1948.

- Chapter Six -

Army Life

During my junior year in high school, World War II continued to rage in the Pacific. Japan continued fighting even though Germany and Italy had surrendered earlier. President Franklin D. Roosevelt had died in office, and Vice President Harry Truman sat in the Oval Office. He was the only person that knew that the United States had developed a weapon capable of killing hundreds of thousands of people in one blast. President Truman continually warned Japanese citizens and leaders that unless Japan surrendered, that weapon would be used. Japan did not heed the warning.

In August of 1945, a few weeks before I started my senior year, atomic bombs were dropped on the Japanese cities of Hiroshima and Nagasaki. Approximately 240,000 Japanese people were killed. On August 15, 1945, the Japanese government finally notified the United States of their surrender. The long, deadly war, taking the lives of more than four hundred thousand American service members, as well as wounding nearly six hundred and seventy-five thousand, was finally over. From our little Arlene church alone, Darwin Aten and Merton Talsma lost their lives, while Freddy Poll was badly wounded and suffered permanent brain damage.

Although Japan had officially surrendered, some Japanese soldiers, sailors, and airmen on remote Pacific islands did not know the war was over. Without communication or commanding officers, they waited in the jungles and mountains for attacks that never came. It was months, and even years before some of them realized hostilities were over. In the meantime, these armed individuals remained a threat to American military personnel. Consequently, President Truman did not declare World War II over until December 31, 1946. That is the reason those of us who enlisted in the summer of 1946 are classified as World War II veterans. Nevertheless, if it had not been for the invention of the atomic bomb, all of us boys in my class might have been caught up in the middle of a bloodbath of immense consequences.

Regardless of the fact that the Japanese military had suffered defeat after defeat, Japanese officials had planned to arm women and children in a last-ditch effort to defend its homeland. An invasion of the Japan mainland under those conditions would have led to unimaginable losses of both Japanese and American lives. As deadly as it was in terms of casualties, the atomic bombing of Hiroshima and Nagasaki would have been minor as compared to a Japanese mainland invasion.

As we graduated from Manton High School, the Class of 1946 left a legacy and a State Class C Basketball Championship trophy. It was a trophy earned by a team that had no stars.

Throughout, various players earned high point honors, and working together as a unit was our highest priority. As we graduated from Manton High School, we were faced with an uncertain future, however.

During our senior year, several of us had been ordered to report to Detroit for an army physical examination. Along with others, I had passed my physical and had been classified as 1-A. That meant that I could be called to active duty at any time.

Meanwhile, the Soviet Union and the United States were on the threshold of war over the occupation of various European nations. There was, also, the issue of the G.I. Bill of Rights. If I enlisted for eighteen months, most of my college expenses would be paid. Those benefits would expire if I entered the military after December 31, 1946. Furthermore, with memories of older basketball and baseball teammates coming home from war killed or wounded, we felt it was our duty to serve our nation.

I enlisted in June but was not called to report until October 1, 1946. I was processed through Fort Sheridan, Illinois, and sent to Fort Dix, New Jersey, for basic training.

Seven From Area Enlist in Army

Seven local youths, six graduating from the 1946 class at Manton, have enlisted in the army to beat the deadline on G.I. Bill of Rights benefits.

According to S/Sgt. John H. Weed, local recruiting officer, those enlisting were Herbert VanHassel, 17, Kenwood Park, Cadillac; Donald L. Alger, 19, Route 2, Manton; Melvin J. Carpenter, 18, Manton; Donald K. Shine, 18, 713 East Chapin Street; Jim L. Baily, 18, Route 2, Manton; Duane R. Grant, 18, Route 1, Manton; and Edward R. Sprik, 18, Manton.

The group was sent to Detroit for final examination and were then sent to Fort Sheridan, Illinois for assignment.

Basic training was going well, and because of my marching skills, which I had learned in marching band, I was appointed squad leader. The daily grind of marching put too much stress on my hernia, however, and I was forced to report to medical services. I was soon in surgery at the base hospital.

The surgery did not go well. There were serious issues with the anesthesia (I intermittently woke up to severe pain), and the procedure brought about hurried discussions, at least when I was awake. At completion of surgery, I discovered that I was in intensive care. After most of the intense pain had subsided and before being sent back to active duty, I was able to procure a three-day pass. Fort Dix was seventy-two miles from New York City. I had heard about the many attractions in that legendary city. I was not disappointed.

After obtaining information as to the locations of the various attractions, I ventured forth. Number one on my list was the Empire State Building. After the accident when a man fell off my dad's windmill, I had never looked forward to climbing high places, and I hesitated as to going to the top of this skyscraper. Even at that young age, however, I realized it would be unwise to run away from fear. I entered the building and got on the elevator.

At the present time, a glass enclosure around the top of the building prevents people from accidently or purposely going over the edge. But that was not the case in 1946. Only a three-foot wall prevented total disaster. I was absolutely amazed by the fantastic view of the surrounding area, but I didn't go near the low barrier.

I had also placed "ice skating show" on my to-do list. Surprisingly, there would be a matinee performance. Seating was like that of a movie theatre, but instead of a screen, there was a sizeable ice rink. As might be expected, the ice show was performed by professional skaters of the highest talent. The performers were equal to anything I had ever imagined, and it was live, right before my eyes—a once-in-a-lifetime experience.

As long as I was in New York City, I didn't want to miss a visit to the grand lady, the Statue of Liberty. Boarding a ferry, along with other visitors, we pulled up on the small island that hosts this symbol of democracy. As I write this, I think about my grandparents steaming into New York Harbor, looking for a land of opportunity. Even if they had been close enough to see the classic engraving on the statue, they wouldn't have been able to read it, since they could not read or write a word of English.

"Give me your tired, your poor, your huddled masses yearning to breathe free, the wretched refuse of your teeming shore. Send these, the homeless, tempest-tost to me. I lift my lamp beside the golden door." – Emma Lazarus. Fitting words for my Grandpa and Grandma Aten.

I climbed the spiral staircase as high as I was allowed to go. Repairs were being made to the torch area and visitors were not permitted at that level.

While exploring Times Square, I came across a large sign reading,

"Jack Dempsey's." Growing up, I had followed the professional boxing scene in the newspapers. Heavyweight title bouts were also broadcast over the radio. Although Jack Dempsey was from an earlier era, he was generally considered to be the greatest heavyweight champion of all time. Peering across Broadway Avenue at the inviting sign, I reasoned that such a legendary figure like Dempsey wouldn't waste time sitting at a bar table.

Later, I learned that Jack Dempsey spent his days at his business place, visiting with customers and signing autographs. I had missed an opportunity to exchange greetings with one of the all-time legendary sports figures.

Continuing to patrol the streets of the Big Apple, I came to a rest under a theatre marquee. Gazing around, I finally realized this was a type of theatre where actors performed live. Across the marquee were the words "John Raitt," "Jan Clayton" in "Carousel." I had not heard of either actor, and the name of the show was new to me. Furthermore, I did not know that a carousel was another name for merry-go-round.

There was to be a matinee performance that very day. I realized the significance of the situation. Opportunities for a person from Michigan to take in live theatre were nearly nonexistent, if not entirely so. I bought a ticket.

The theatre was in a semi-circle, and I looked down on the stage. The dialog was difficult for me to understand, but the singing was quite spectacular. Except for singers I had enjoyed over the radio, I had never heard such voices.

During my stay in the hospital and my rehab, my unit had completed basic training and had been sent to Japan as a part of the Army of Occupation. Instead of sending me back to basic training, the officer in charge sent me to a hospital base near Boston, where I was issued a .45-caliber handgun along with a military police armband. It was quickly learned that I could type and compose letters. I was put behind a desk with a typewriter. Later, I was assigned to duty as a guard at the main gate, and finally, I put in some duty on the prison ward. Eventually, my inability to adjust to military life caught up with me, however.

After a glorious escapade, upon which I will not elaborate, a superior army official requested that I retire from the military police and seek more suitable work. In plain English, I was "kicked out" and reassigned to the glorious task of washing dishes in the mess hall. My stay in the base kitchen was short-lived, however.

"The major wants to see you." It was a noncommissioned officer assigned to the mess hall. I had no idea as to what it was about. The major, whom I had never met, was a soft-spoken man who appeared near retirement age. He told me he had learned about my clerical skills, and that I would be in charge of all civilian employee time records, a very important job. Later, I was assigned to the kiosk at the mess hall entrance during noon hour to assist a nonmilitary woman with financial records as to officer meals. This was in addition to my duties keeping re-

Army days. Served from October 1, 1946, until March 28, 1948.

Army Life

cords regarding civilian employees, of which there were hundreds, as I recall.

As was common practice in army installations, enlisted men at our base, known as Murphy General Hospital, slept in large rooms known as barracks. Bunk beds were close together, allowing for no more than a footlocker between them. Married men lived off base.

If the person next to you snored loudly, you were in for a long night. Not just "a night," but seven nights a week. Here and there, a person who seemed to detest showers would occupy a bunk. If that person was next to you, you prayed for his early discharge from service.

Although my skills were highly desired in the military, and the duties I performed exceeded the abilities of those ranked well above me, I encountered problems when off duty. When my daily duties were completed, I regularly exited out the main gate.

As I neared my discharge date, I became involved in a fiasco that I feared might lead to a court-martial. For those unfamiliar with military law, the offender appears in a military court before a military judge. The results of a court-martial do not usually end in the offender's favor. The judge might sentence the offender to military jail or even prison if the offense is bad enough. Or, the judge might order the offender immediately discharged from service with a dishonorable discharge or a discharge known as a "blue deuce," unfit for military duty.

My predicament was brought on by a situation where my common sense was replaced by wishful thinking. One afternoon, a soldier from my barracks whose name was Hamilton approached me, asking me to accompany him into Boston that same evening. He said that the officer in charge of the mess hall (my boss) had given him car keys and told him to take the vehicle assigned to the mess hall (food service). When I questioned Hamilton, he responded by showing me the car keys.

If Hamilton had been a buck private, I undoubtedly would have declined the offer. Hamilton, however, had attained some rank.

I do not remember the errands we were supposed to complete, but before long we were at a roller-skating rink. After an hour or so of skating, we started to leave the parking lot, and Hamilton bumped another car. Someone wrote down our license plate number. As Hamilton turned into the main gate, the military police were waiting for us. They took us into custody. Hamilton had lied to me about being given permission to use an army vehicle, and he had sneaked into, or broken into, the main office and had stolen the car keys.

Hamilton lost his rank and was busted down to buck private. His stripes were removed from his field jacket and shirts. He was given other punishments.

I was allowed to keep my corporal stripes, but I was required to shovel coal in the heating plant for three long weekends. I pondered the difference in punishment for Hamilton and for myself. I finally figured out the reason Hamilton got busted and I did not was because Hamilton was the perpetrator of the mess, whereas I was simply empty-headed. The army can bust or prosecute an offender for stealing as in Hamilton's case, but the army can't bust a person for stupidity. If so, from my observations, the army would have a lot more buck privates.

One might think that a person almost totally deprived of money growing up would want to hold onto every penny available. If a person never has money, however, that person often never learns to manage available funds. That was certainly true in my case. So, on the occasions I would get a furlough, I never had money for transportation home. The only alternative was to hitchhike. There was one exception, however. We could ride free on a military aircraft if there was a flight going in the right direction. On one occasion, I hopped a plane at Springfield, Massachusetts, and flew to Dayton, Ohio. That put me within 150 miles from the Michigan state line, a significant assist. When hitchhiking, I often rode in semis.

On one occasion, hitchhiking from my Manton home to Waltham, Massachusetts, my home base, my progress was terribly slow and I ran out of money just as I crossed the state line into Indiana. I had not eaten since I left Manton, as I recall, and I was hoping to catch a ride in a semi to the East Coast.

As I stood thumbing along the expressway, the cold night air was penetrating through my field jacket, and I shivered as I watched one vehicle after another pass by. The lights of a small town appeared in the distance, and eventually I decided to seek shelter. A small hotel was located just within the village limits, and I entered the door. A gentleman of thirty or so years of age staffed the desk. "Can I help you?" he asked. "I'm looking for a place to sleep," I replied. "But, I don't have any money."

After discussing alternatives with the clerk, I was able to reverse charges on a telephone call to my parents, after which my dad wired me a sum of money to cover my room rent and railroad fare to Boston. Unfortunately, I underestimated the railroad fare, and I was forced to get off the train in a small town about seventy miles from Boston. As I recall, I still had not eaten since leaving home.

Leaving the small town station and preparing to hitchhike the remainder of the distance to the base, I passed the window of a hole-in-the-wall bakery with a lunch counter. In the window I spotted a large, candy-coated doughnut. I went in and sat at the counter. A little man, speaking broken English, asked, "Can I help you?"

"I'll have a cup of coffee and that doughnut in the window," I replied.

As I finished the doughnut, the little man said, "That will be fifteen cents."

"I don't have any money," I replied. "But I'll send you the money when I get back to the base." He quickly assured me that I should not worry about paying. I thanked him profusely, promised to send him the money (didn't happen), and hitchhiked back to the base.

Since I am often not very wary of consequences of my actions, others might hope there would be a lesson in all of this that might be of benefit to me. I am hoping for that, as well.

On the twenty-eighth day of March 1948, I left the army separation center, received my honorable discharge and two hundred dollars mustering-out pay, walked out the main gate, and hitchhiked back to Manton.

I was not really the type of person suited for military life, and my social anxiety issues were difficult to overcome. I did, however, honorably serve my country, and that is something I'll never regret.

Spending time with dad in garden of Manton home after military time.

- Chapter Seven -

College, Football, and … Marriage

Unlike my enlistment in the army, which had been a rather sudden decision, the pathway to my enrollment as a student in Western Michigan College, later renamed Western Michigan University, had a starting point many years earlier. Early in my grade school days, I had become keenly interested in all types of athletics. That interest only intensified as I entered high school.

World War II was raging and throughout the United States, public schools were encouraged to establish boys' fitness programs to prepare young men for future military service. As a part of our training, obstacle courses were set up on a playground and close order drill was taught in the gymnasium. I enjoyed those activities immensely.

Then, late one afternoon in May of 1944, as I walked up the hill toward the locker room following high school baseball practice, a sudden realization crossed my mind. If I enjoy baseball and other sports along with fitness classes to this extent, why don't I become a physical education teacher and coach. After that epiphany, the idea of pursuing any other vocation rarely occurred to me. At about that same time, I learned about a highly esteemed men's physical education program offered at Western Michigan College.

Shortly after my return to Manton after my army discharge, I made contact with the Veterans Administration in order to activate my G.I. Bill benefits. I was told that I would receive approximately one hundred dollars per month for living expenses, and that my tuition and books would be covered by the Veterans Administration.

Freshman orientation at Western Michigan went on for a week, during which time I signed up for classes, picked up my required textbooks and, through the Dean of Students Office, found a rooming house near campus where I could rent a room for five dollars per week.

Of the four students in the rooming house, three of us were veterans. When one graduated, another veteran moved in. Because of our military service, we had a sense of camaraderie.

Shortly after beginning classes, I responded to an invitation on the gymnasium bulletin board to try out for the freshman football team. Under collegiate rules at the time, freshmen were not allowed to play on varsity teams. Running out on the practice field for the first time, I estimated about one hundred thirty freshmen in pads. I learned later that many of them had been recruited by various coaches. I was not one of those recruited, but I was not deterred.

My football status at that time was what is now known as a "walk-on." Athletic Department policy at that time was to allow anyone to try out for any athletic team. Consequently, many of us were more or less tolerated. We were not expected to ever have much of an impact on the varsity team.

As the first game of the freshman football schedule approached, I learned that it would be an away game, and that the traveling team members' names would be posted on the locker room bulletin board. I was disappointed to discover that my name was not included. I approached Mr. Slaughter, the head freshman coach, and asked if there had been some mistake—had my name been accidently omitted.

"No Sprik, there has been no mistake. Most of the players on the traveling squad have been recruited. They are mostly all-state, or at least all-conference honored players. People like you don't have much of a chance against players at that level. I suggest that you drop out of football and concentrate on your studies."

Growing up in what would now be considered as "poverty," I suffered through many nights in severe pain due to lack of dental and medical care. I had also fought back against sexual assault by an older neighborhood boy. Unlike many other players brought up in privilege, I had always been "rowing against the waves." I can't think of anything Coach Slaughter could have told me that would have been more motivational. "Well," I thought, "we'll see about that."

During the summer following my freshman year, and while living with my widowed mother in Lake City, Michigan, I eagerly picked up our mail each day, hoping for an invitation to varsity football camp. I was not optimistic, however, as I had played very little on the freshman team. But, one day in July, the mail included an envelope with a return address labeled Western Michigan College. Anxiously, I opened the letter. It was an invitation to early football camp. I was euphoric.

It was mid-August. We were housed in a men's dormitory and were treated royally. Breakfast, lunch, and dinner were cafeteria style and food was unlimited. The head trainer and his assistant handled wounds and other injuries with great care.

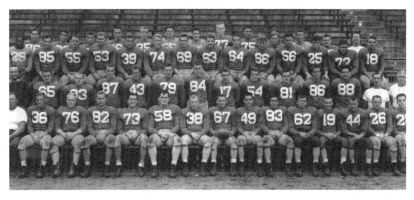

Sophomore football season, Reg Sprik near center of back row.

At the beginning of football camp, I was in the fourth string. But it wasn't long before I caught the attention of the coaching staff. During drills and scrimmages, my speed and quickness created problems for the veteran first string players, and they had problems blocking me.

The first game of the season was at home against a team from Iowa. During the fourth quarter of that game, I was utterly shocked when a coach came up to me and said, "Sprik, you're going in at right defensive tackle." That is now known as "the blind side." I was somewhat surprised that I performed quite well.

DRINK
Coca-Cola
REG. U.S. PAT. OFF.

1949 WESTERN MICHIGAN ROSTER

NO.	NAME	POS.	AGE	WT.	HT.	HOME	LETTERS
17	Thompson, Arnold	RH	21	165	5-11	Yale	0
18	Gratton, Leslie	RH	24	180	5-9	Flint	3
19	Stull, Richard	RH	24	170	5-11	Chicago, Ill.	1
23	Johnston, Len	Q	21	164	5-10	Saginaw	0
25	Flaherty, William	Q	19	170	5-11	Benton Harbor	0
26	Harris, Norman	Q	26	183	5-9	Chicago, Ill.	1
28	Dunn, George	Q	25	180	6-3	Birmingham	3
33	Wright, Donald	FB	19	178	5-8	Kalamazoo	0
36	Hildreth, Harry	FB	25	195	6-1	Flint	3
38	Hartman, Lloyd	FB	25	210	6-0	Battle Creek	3
39	Broda, Gene	FB	22	195	5-10	Chicago, Ill.	0
41	Waterloo, Jerry	LH	21	156	6-0	Richmond	0
42	Holloway, John	LH	22	160	5-8	Chicago, Ill.	0
43	White, Robert	LH	23	178	6-1	Muskegon	3
44	Snow, Richard	LH	23	170	5-9	Chicago, Ill.	0
46	Morse, Robert	LH	20	165	5-9	Caseville	0
49	Bauer, Ted	LH	24	178	6-0	Kalamazoo	3
48	Walterhouse, Bob	LH	21	160	5-9	Ann Arbor	1
52	Doxey, Homer	C	22	175	5-6	Kalamazoo	1
53	Merritt, Hobart	C	27	219	6-2	Osceola Mills, Pa.	0
54	Earle, Courval	C	21	190	6-0	Plainwell	0
55	Green, James	C	24	194	5-11	Flint	0
56	Tomanek, Emil	C	22	190	6-0	Cicero, Ill.	0
58	Schoolmaster, Charles	C	24	240	6-4	Kalamazoo	3
61	Rossi, Arthur	G	19	175	5-10	Farmington	0
62	Contes, Tom	G	25	200	5-10	Chicago, Ill.	2
63	Avronvo, Eli	G	21	178	5-11	Kalamazoo	0
64	Van Laanen, Pete	G	21	168	5-10	Iron Mountain	0
65	Dyas, George	G	24	161	5-10	Battle Creek	0
66	Tuma, John	G	23	185	5-9	Berwyn, Ill.	1
67	Carlson, Robert (Capt.)	G	24	185	5-10	Kingsford	3
68	Leeson, Glen	G	24	178	5-10	Crown Pt. Ind.	0
69	Duditch, George	G	26	180	5-11	Detroit	1
71	Decker, Lawrence	T	19	225	5-9	Buchanan	0
72	Sprik, Reg	T	21	190	6-0	Manton	0
73	Micatrotto, Al	T	23	210	6-2	Cleveland, O.	3
74	Stanley, Roland	T	20	200	5-11	Lansing	0
75	Duhan, Robert	T	20	210	6-1	Paw Paw	0
76	Pearson, Mal	T	26	220	6-0	Chicago, Ill.	3
77	Kennedy, Tom	T	19	190	6-2	Niles	0
78	Fleming, William	T	20	205	5-10	Detroit	0
79	Pitkin, William	T	22	215	6-2	Brighton	0
81	Morris, Tom	E	19	165	5-10	Valparaiso, Ind.	0
82	Mesko, George	E	25	210	6-4	Milan	2
83	Zabonick, Pat	E	22	195	5-10	Coldwater	1
84	Clysdale, Pat	E	20	190	6-3	Detroit	0
85	Vanzo, Arnold	E	21	170	5-10	Dearborn	0
86	Cater, Alvia	E	19	170	6-0	Muskegon Ht.	0
87	Brisendine, Jake	E	18	170	6-2	Flint	0
88	Green, Robert	E	20	180	6-1	Alma	0

Student Manager- Robert Brown, St. Clair

Making the roster of a college football team was the culmination of a longtime dream.

I didn't play in the next game against the University of Cincinnati and suspected that I might now and then see some playing time. The third game during that sophomore year was a home game and it was homecoming weekend at Western. The night before the game, I witnessed the annual huge bonfire with a raucous crowd and cheerleaders hyping up the crowd. Members of the alumni had returned and there was much ado on campus.

As we put on pads for the game, a rumor came around to me suggesting that I was in the starting lineup. It was beyond my belief, and I considered it just foolish hearsay. I learned that my two older brothers had driven down from Lake City to see the game.

We stood at attention as "The Star Spangled Banner" played and the American flag rose to the top of the stadium flagpole. The public address announcer then went to the starting lineups and each starting player ran out onto the field as his name was called. It is impossible to describe the emotional jolt I felt as my name rang out across Waldo Stadium and as I ran out on the field in front of my family members and a wildly cheering homecoming crowd. From my early days, playing alone kicking a beat-up football up and down a two-track road and imagining just such a moment, and now this.

At the annual football banquet the following spring, George Dunn, a senior defensive back, received the award as Most Valuable Player, and the coaches selected me for the Most Improved Player Award.

Appropriate Gesture
Over 345 Attend Annual Bronco Football Banquet
By Bob Wagner

Western Michigan College's annual football banquet, sponsored by the athletic board of the institution, was a success from principal speaker to Swiss steak last night.

Over 345 persons were in attendance in Walwood Hall ballroom to witness the final tribute of the season to Western's football and cross country squads, and to bid farewell to 15 seniors.

Flurry of Anecdotes

The program moved at a rapid gait, thanks to the able toast master job accomplished by Herbert W. (Buck) Read, former head basketball coach at Western. And the anecdotes of Principal Speaker Lyall Smith, sports editor of the Detroit Free Press, helped the patrons to digest their meal with ease.

Special awards were made to two Western gridders for their contribution on the field of action in 1949. George Dunn, a senior and defensive quarterback, was voted the most valuable player by his teammates.

And Ed Sprik of Manton, Mich., was selected as the most improved player of the season by the Bronco football coaching staff. Sprik was a sophomore tackle.

TUESDAY, DECEMBER 6, 1949.   KALAMAZOO GAZETTE Photo
WESTERN GRIDDERS RECEIVE SPECIAL AWARDS FROM JOHN C. HOEKJE
George Dunn (left), Most Valuable; Reg Sprik, Most Improved Player

College football players have little free time. I could not take a class that started later than one o'clock since a two o'clock class might not dismiss quite on time and I might not make it to the locker room by three o'clock, an absolute requirement.

College, Football, and ... Marriage

Most of the time I would be out of the locker room by 6 p.m., at which time I would join other players in a trek to the Student Union for our evening meal. A considerable variety of food was available cafeteria style, and we were allowed to eat as much as we could put away.

Leaving the cafeteria and walking to my room, I would be fortunate if I could get there before 7 p.m. Since I could not take late afternoon classes, I was forced to begin classes at 8 a.m. No studying would have been done for the following morning 8 a.m. class or other classes to follow. Exhausted, I often tried to sleep an hour or so, wake up and study until midnight. The next day would be a repeat.

We traveled by bus in those days. Most of our away games were in other states, as far away as Missouri. We usually left on Friday morning and arrived back on campus Sunday evening. Occasionally, we left on Thursday morning. Monday morning quizzes were dreaded.

As to a college football player's social life, it is well described by a quote from an unknown player, "It is definitely a lot, especially midterm and finals week. It's about understanding when you get home from practice and you are really tired, and you don't want to do anything, having that discipline to do what you need to do. It's learning to say 'no' to going to social events. People hit you up and you have to tell them 'not right now'".

As my sophomore year was coming to a close, I learned that the City of Manton planned to hire a swimming instructor and lifeguard for Lake Billings, the local hangout for kids of all ages. I applied for the job. City Commissioners obviously remembered me from my State Championship Basketball days, and I was soon hired. There was a qualification, however.

I would need to attend and graduate from the ten-day Red Cross Water Safety School at White Lake, near Whitehall, before starting the job. All expenses would be paid by the City of Manton.

Training at the water safety school was intense, to say the least. Classes included first aid and boating (tipping over boats and canoes in the middle of White Lake, climbing back into the craft and hand paddling to shore). We learned the reverse side stroke, which was absolutely essential. We had to swim one-hundred yards continuously with each of the basic swimming strokes. We also learned to release underwater death grips, get the drowning victim under control, and bring the victim to shore. Classes started at 8 a.m. and concluded at 6 p.m. for ten straight days, including Saturday and Sunday.

Nearly all participants had jobs waiting for them when the Red Cross Water Safety School ended. Meanwhile, various instructors kept reminding us that some people might not pass the final swimming and lifesaving tests. In the end, everyone passed the final examination and received certification as a Red Cross Water Safety Instructor.

Graduating from the Red Cross Water Safety School at White Lake.
Reg Sprik back row center.

In retrospect, I came to realize that all our instructors were determined to make sure none of his or her students would fail in a lifesaving situation. After completion of the water safety school, I experienced a deep sense of gratitude toward the dedicated water safety instructors. I was exceptionally well prepared to take over the swimming and lifesaving instructor position at Lake Billings, as well as elsewhere.

Lake Billings is created by a dam that, at one time, supplied electricity for the City of Manton. Because of the constant water exchange from Cedar Creek, Lake Billings is chilly in the mornings before the sun warms up the water. Consequently, I started swimming and lifesaving classes beginning at 1 p.m. I taught beginning, intermediate, and advanced swimming classes, as well as junior and senior lifesaving classes. Once or twice a week, in the evening, adult women took a beginning swimmer class.

When my junior football season began, Coach Gill made an inexplicable decision. He removed me from my defensive tackle position, where I had excelled and received special honors, and tried to install me in an offensive position I had never before played. During a practice drill new to me, I was seriously injured and missed nearly the entire season.

Because of costs to the Athletic Department, injured football players do not travel to away games. Such was the case during my junior year when I had been seriously injured in practice. A torn abdominal muscle sheath had been slow to heal. One other player, Benny Decker, was also on the injured list and was also left in Kalamazoo.

For a change, I casually checked the College Calendar of Events. I took note of a dance to be held at the Student Union and there would be a live band. Out of boredom, I called Benny Decker on the phone to ask if he wanted to meet me there that Saturday night. He did.

Sitting off to the side, we listened to the band and observed the whirl of humanity. Unexpectedly, a dancing pair of girls passed by on the outside. One was very attractive. I asked Decker if we should split the pair of dancers. He agreed. Hurriedly, I headed straight for the one that caught my eye. We danced away the rest of the evening.

She was driving her dad's car and she agreed to drop me off at the local nightclub, Club Hollywood, after the dance. I told her I would get a ride home. By that time, my bachelorhood was pretty well established, and I simply went on to other things. But serendipity entered the picture.

On a whim and because of a monthly paycheck, I had signed up with the campus R.O.T.C. I had failed to consider the end result. Upon graduation, I would be required to serve two years on active duty. I had already served an enlistment of eighteen months, and I did not desire further military service. Nevertheless, I had not yet been able to undo my R.O.T.C. commitment, and the formal military ball was upcoming. We were strongly urged to be there. Unfortunately, I couldn't think of anyone who might be my dancing partner.

"Why don't you ask that girl that dropped you off at Club Hollywood?" It was a suggestion from a guy in my rooming house.

For some reason, I did not think of that lovely lady. I found her phone number and extended my invitation. She accepted. At the last minute, however, I found myself in a serious jam. Earlier in the week, I had dropped off my military trousers at the dry cleaners, and I had neglected to pick them up. Full military dress was required for this formal event. I visualized myself

Marilyn Carlson, my military ball date.

flitting around the dance floor with no pants! Not a pretty picture.

By the time I realized my mistake, the dry cleaning establishment had closed for the day. With no alternative, I desperately called the various men's dormitories seeking an R.O.T.C. guy who was not attending the dance. Finally, my call was returned by a "Good Samaritan" about my size. I rushed to the dorm, dressed, and met my date barely on time. Her name was Marilyn Carlson.

Marilyn was a freshman at Western and lived near the outer edge of Kalamazoo. She was an only child. There was a recreation room in the basement of her home, and I began to visit her there on a regular basis. Her parents were gracious and had no objections to my visits.

Returning to my summer waterfront job at Manton after my junior year at Western Michigan College, I decided to use my morning to organize kid's ball games at the school playground. Kids didn't have much to do and there was a good response. We played sides and sometimes a game called Workup.

In the meantime, some junior high and high school girls who didn't have to work expressed an interest in forming a softball team. Practice was organized and a couple of young married women joined the team.

Games were scheduled against various women's teams and local merchants bought uniforms for the team. Even to this day, I'm occasion-

Mantonettes Women's Softball Team
Front row l to r: *Dorothy Swanson, Janet Beaver, Annette Dontje,*
Boots Haveman, Star Bridson. **Back row l to r:** *Janice Johnston, Phyllis Norman,*
Florence Dontje, unidentified, Louise Elliot, Gail Fewlass, Joann Fewlass.
(Photo courtesy of Janice Johnston-Zuder)

ally reminded of that team. A few team members are still around.

And now, I began to miss seeing Marilyn on a regular basis. I was a military veteran, had been out of high school for four years and had dated various girls during that time, some for a period of time. This time, however, something was different. My feelings for Marilyn were much deeper, and I realized that this was the girl I wanted for my life partner.

August 24, 1951, our wedding day.

After several invitations to visit me at Lake City throughout early summer of 1950, Marilyn finally made her way north to Lake City in early July. My mother provided a room for her. While we were out for a drive, I parked the vehicle in downtown Cadillac. Leaving Marilyn in the car, I walked to Sandy's Jewelry Store. While there, I bought an engagement ring, returned to the car, and presented the ring to Marilyn. Being a quiet, reserved individual, Marilyn simply took the ring and put it on her finger.

Rather quickly, we decided we did not want to marry during the school year. The summer of the following year, we decided, was too long to wait. We would set the wedding date for late in the next month, August 24.

Marilyn's parents were not church people, so the wedding was planned for the Kalamazoo First Christian Reformed Church where I was a member. Marilyn's mother soon became busy with details. The wedding and reception was a nice event, and Marilyn and I took off on our honeymoon with my cousin's borrowed car and a fifty dollar bill in my wallet.

We drove north to the Upper Peninsula, but we soon ran out of money. With barely enough cash to return to Lake City, I spent the rest of our honeymoon shoveling coal in a coal yard and residing in my mother's house.

As the semester started, following our wedding, we rented a studio apartment near the college with my G.I. Bill income and Marilyn's job in a local bank. Due to poor grades, resulting from my social life with Marilyn, I had become ineligible for the football season. Concentrating on my studies, I was able to bring my grades back up and prepare to complete my college football career the following year.

In July 1952, following our August 1951 wedding, we welcomed a six-pound, six-ounce new member into our household. We named him David Edward. Edward was the name handed down from his grandfather and his dad.

By this time, I was becoming disenchanted with the way the football program was being run and I made contact with the coaching staff at the University of Michigan. Considering my experience, the University of Michigan coaches were very welcoming.

At that time, a college transfer would have meant a loss of credits and a delayed graduation, however. I was now married with a child and finances were a serious issue. Furthermore, my G.I. benefits might have expired before my graduation. A transfer did not seem logical.

Although I didn't realize it at the time, the Western Michigan College coaching staff was beginning its last year. That came as no surprise to past and present players. In that last season, I was again moved to a new position I had never before played. Al Manne, an all-city fullback at Grand Rapids Union High School, was removed from the backfield, where he was badly needed, and moved to a pulling guard spot while I occupied the other pulling guard position.

Wearing number 79 and downfield blocking from a pulling guard position in senior football season.

Bruce Bosma, the Muskegon Flying Dutchman, carrying the ball for a ten-yard gain. Moving up to lead the way for Bosma is Reg Sprik, one of the Broncos hard blocking guards. Moving in fast to make the tackle is Don Link, speedy Illinois Wesleyan halfback, who scored the Titans only touchdown early in the game on a breath-taking 88-yard kickoff return. This is one of the many thrilling long gains performed by the Broncos throughout the afternoon.

College football was going through many changes involving varying offensive and defensive alignments. Our coaching staff was totally unprepared for the changes, and we suffered an embarrassing loss to Miami of Ohio.

REG SPRIK ON VARSITY TEAM

Kalamazoo — Reg Sprik, son of Mrs. Ed Sprik, Lake City, Mich., is a member of the 1952 varsity football team, here, at Western Michigan College.

Sprik, a senior, is one of the very few individuals who never played high school football, but later proved to be a standout college gridiron star. As a freshman and sophomore here, he played tackle but last year never played. Sprik is now working at offensive guard where he has landed a starting spot on the first team.

He is a former graduate of Manton High School, where he was a very fine athlete in basketball and baseball for four years.

College, Football, and … Marriage

Over time we eventually were able to move into campus housing for married students, and I seriously considered staying on campus to complete a master's degree. But, one day as Marilyn and I discussed future plans, I asked her, "How much money do we have?"

"I don't have any," she replied. "How much money do you have?"

I reached in my pocket and pulled out a nickel. "This is it," I said. Financial circumstances had never been quite this bad. We had no money for food. A master's degree was out of the question.

Fortunately, there was a small supply of gas in the fuel tank of our vehicle. Desperately, I went to various banks in the city, trying to borrow some survival money. Eventually, a sympathetic loan officer let me have fifty dollars.

Graduation Day

In January 1953, I graduated with a bachelor of science degree and a teaching certificate. Through the college placement office, I had been offered a teaching and coaching job at Wyandotte Roosevelt High School in Wyandotte, Michigan. Even though I did not want a career working in the Detroit area, our financial situation led me to accepting the position.

Because of World War II veterans returning to civilian life and marrying, there was a critical housing shortage in Wyandotte, and Marilyn and I could not find affordable housing. Consequently, Marilyn and our new son stayed in Kalamazoo with her parents while I stayed in a rooming house in Wyandotte and returned to Kalamazoo on weekends.

- Chapter Eight -

Growing Family and Career Changes

My teaching and coaching contract with the Wyandotte School System was expiring and I had signed a contract to teach elementary physical education and high school United States history at Lake City Public Schools. My contract also required me to be head coach of all athletic teams. For health reasons, the head of the football program was retiring, and the head basketball coach had moved on.

During the year prior to my hiring, neither the varsity football nor varsity basketball team had won a single game. The only thing lower than Lake City football and basketball scores was the morale of the student athletes.

We lived in Lake City from the summer of 1953 until the winter of 1959. During that time, I made several career changes. The highlight, by far, of our six-year stay in that community, however, turned out to be the expansion of our family from three to six members.

Son Robert Roy (Bob), joined us on February 13, 1954. Bob weighed in at seven-pounds, eight-ounces. On May 21, 1955, our first daughter,

Bob and Dave   *Jan*   *Nancy*

Janice Margaret, appeared on the scene at seven-pounds, two-ounces. Wrapping up the childbearing scene, daughter Nancy Joyce brought it all to an end on May 19, 1958, tipping the scale at eight-pounds, eleven-ounces.

In our early days in Lake City, we bought a beagle pup and named her "Freckles," because of her facial markings. Other very fine dogs became part of our household, but Freckles remained a constant. She lived to be nearly twenty years of age, and throughout her life, she was my hunting companion.

As I began my head coaching journey at Lake City High School, I did so against the advice of the placement director at Western Michigan. He strongly urged me to begin my career as an assistant before accepting a head coaching position. After two years head coaching at Lake City, I fully understood his reasoning.

Over time, most of us who are teaching and coaching young people begin to lose our sharp edges and start to see issues from more than one side. As a four year Division I football player and state basketball champion, however, I expected as much from my players as I expected of myself. Those athletes who shared my competitive fire stayed the course. Those unwilling to give it their all fell by the wayside or were given a choice. My teams were small in number but were single-minded. We began to win games and upset teams that had used Lake City ball clubs as doormats.

During my time at the Lake City School System, I was able to use my influence to start high school boys and high school girls physical education classes. I also began seventh and eighth grade basketball teams and scheduled games. In cooperation with a female staff member, a high school girls' basketball team was formed. Games were scheduled and uniforms obtained.

Lake City Memories

Marilyn and Reg on porch of Lake City home.

Dad (Reg) in front of our Lake City home. Dave and Jan on my right, Bob and Nancy on my left.

(l to r) in front of Lake City home – Bob, Nancy, Jan, and Dave getting ready to hit the road.

Marilyn in front of our Lake City home with (l to r) Dave, Jan, Nancy, and Bob.

(l to r) Bob, Jan, and Dave stare into the bright sun at our Lake City home.

Newest family member, Nancy, is looked after by siblings (l to r) Dave, Jan, and Bob.

My schedule was often tight. I sometimes practiced with the junior high basketball teams after school, rushed home for a quick bite to eat, and then hurried back to the school to catch the bus for an away varsity basketball game. The next morning, I would be teaching a history class.

During my second year at Lake City High School, two similar events occurred that changed the course of my career. In each case, I experienced severe chest pains, and it was believed that I was suffering a heart attack. Tests at the hospital revealed no such thing, however, and I was soon sent home.

The events brought on considerable concern, however. Marilyn and I came to the agreement that my physical issues were probably stress related. Marilyn suggested that I might want to seek a different line of work. I agreed. Later, I came to realize that Marilyn probably considered youthful widowhood with several small children as not being a very promising future.

Marilyn's concern for my health, along with my inability to get a decent raise from the Lake City School District, prompted me to accept a sales position calling on northern Michigan schools. The yearly salary matched that of the local superintendent of schools, and my expense allowance paid for the cost of driving a brand new Chevy station wagon. Furthermore, there was the possibility of a year-end bonus. There was a lot of repetition involved with the work, however, and after a year on the job, I became bored. At that point, the family invited me to work in the local family-owned automobile dealership.

After three years working in various aspects of the car business, I accepted a position selling textbooks to schools throughout much of the state of Michigan. Most of my book business was in southwestern Michigan and we made plans to move to the Grand Rapids area.

During our stay in Lake City, I remained very active in adult basketball and fast-pitch softball. I played softball mainly on lighted fields in

On Lake City porch – back row Grandma (Margaret) Sprik, Marilyn, Reg. Front row (l to r) Bob, Nancy, and Jan.

Dad (Reg) holds Nancy. l to r: Dave, Jan, and Bob in Lake City.

Happy, Happy in Lake City! l to r: Dave, Nancy, Jan, and Bob.

(l to r) in front of Lake City home – Bob, Nancy, Jan, and Dave getting ready to hit the road.

both Cadillac and McBain. Marilyn was my best fan. She greatly enjoyed watching the games.

My job with Lake City Schools involved working summers as a life-guard at the downtown beach. Since I was a Red Cross certified water safety instructor, in addition to guarding the beach, I also taught swimming and lifesaving classes.

Bob and Jan well remember trips to the local Dairy Queen, which was conveniently located about a city block from our Lake City house. Uncle Jay and Margaret Aten owned the ice cream parlor, so our kids could always count on a very full cone.

The small city, known as Lake City, sits on beautiful Lake Missaukee, where much fishing takes place. The best fishing story that I've heard about Lake City, however, took place on dry land. Furthermore, it involved our son, David.

One summer morning, likely a Saturday, son David, always an early riser, appeared at our bedroom door. "I want to go fishing," he told us, "but I don't have a lure."

It was during a time when kids roamed free. Besides, he would be fishing from shore and there was no danger. "Take a dollar from my wallet and buy a lure at the tackle store on your way," I explained.

Following my directions, Dave left the house with rod, reel, and bill in hand. Entering the store, he reviewed and selected a nice-looking lure and paid with the bill. When the store owner returned, he handed Dave the lure and a handful of bills.

With his bonus money, Dave continued ordering lures until the money was gone. Returning home from fishing, Dave showed us his bag full of fishing lures.

A quick check of my wallet revealed the absence of a twenty-dollar bill. Our next activity involved a quick trip to the tackle shop, bag in hand and Dave at my side, for a merchandise return. We learned that, to a six-year-old, a bill is a bill.

- Chapter Nine -

Return to Farm Life and Vacation Adventures

It was our first night in our Ottawa County farmhouse. I stepped out our door and was immediately struck by the silence. There were no sounds of vehicles or other human-created noises. The stars sparkled brightly overhead. In the distance, lighted windows of another farmhouse appeared through the darkness. A sense of peace came over me. Perhaps, in the recesses of my memory, I had returned to the quiet solitude of my childhood home in rural Arlene.

Aerial view of the forty-one acre farm the family lived on for nine years. Jamestown, Michigan.

Because of my sales position with McGraw-Hill Publishing Company, we needed to move from our rented home in Lake City to southwestern Michigan, so I could live near the center of my territory. Subsequently, we temporarily moved to a rented home in Grandville.

During our stay in that location, we made contact with real estate agent Gary, with plans to buy five or ten acres on which to build a house. But our agent had a different idea.

Gary had listed a forty-one-acre farm with a sizeable house, described in earlier times as an upright and lean-to. It was covered with Insulbrick, and a nice barn came with the property. Gary urged us to buy it. The price was extremely reasonable. The purchase required only three thousand dollars down, and we could buy on a land contract.

We drove out to look over the property. Marilyn reluctantly agreed to make the purchase, and we immediately set about to try to borrow the three-thousand-dollar down payment. Fortunately, family and relatives came through for us, and between Christmas and New Year's Day of 1960–61, we moved in.

l to r: Jan, Nancy, Polly (Marilyn's dog), Marilyn, Bob on his horse, Candy, Dutchie, Dave, Freckles.

Soon after our arrival, livestock began to populate our farm. Three horses and a Shetland pony served as transportation for the young of the family, as well as free rides for visiting friends. Two hundred white leghorn chickens came aboard, so Marilyn, at that time a stay-at-home mom, could earn spending money with a Saturday egg route.

Two young calves we purchased from a neighbor became immediately sick and had to be nursed back to health by moving them to the basement of our house. They continued to prosper until it was time to move them to a farm where facilities were better suited for their continued growth.

But as small egg farmers began to give way to large egg "factories," prices for eggs began to drop, and the cost of chicken feed started to rise sharply. We were losing money with our leghorn chickens and were forced to sell them. Since we had a sizeable facility for chickens, we decided to take a different approach.

We had visited fairs where we had seen a large variety of exotic chickens of various breeds. Some had top knots, some had long beautiful tails, and some laid colored "Easter eggs." The young birds we ordered from the hatchery soon grew to adult size and we began showing them at fairs throughout southwestern Michigan. As chickens were judged at these fairs, we accumulated blue, white, and red ribbons, plus cash awards. At the Ionia Fair, we received a check for nearly one hundred and fifty dollars, a week's wages in those days.

Our two young goats kept us entertained with their climbing antics. On one occasion, we had positioned a steel trash barrel against the lower level of our utility shed which was attached to the house. The arrangement served as nothing less than a nifty ladder for the two adventurous members of our livestock family. One day, when we returned from the store, we were startled to discover the two scalawags standing on the peak of our farmhouse roof. On another occasion, we needed to rescue them when they had somehow climbed out on the narrow limb of a sloping tree and seemed unable to get back down.

Most years, we bought young pigs and raised them to market size, about two hundred pounds. Much of their feed came from pigweeds we pulled from behind the barn, which made the hog situation a profitable endeavor, and provided meat for our dinner table. Very briefly, there were also a few sheep in residence. Each of our daughters had a pet lamb.

A low-lying area on the east side of our square-shaped forty acres was converted to a miniature pond, deep enough for swimming and for hosting a few rainbow trout. There were no places to swim in our geographical location, and the pond allowed for cooling off on hot summer days.

l to r: Marilyn at grill, Jan, Bob, Nancy and Dave enjoy our farm pond on homemade raft.

Shortly after arriving at the farm, we began to accumulate farm machinery, most of it used. Equipment included a John Deere B tractor, hay wagon, hay mower, side delivery rake, and manure spreader.

(If there are farm animals on the property, waste disposal is necessary.) All animal waste (manure) went back on the land for fertilizer.

Haying time was a memorable time for the entire family and was, indeed, a family project. Marilyn and our two daughters loved to drive the tractor while Dave, Bob, and I picked up the hay bales and loaded them on the wagon. Finding a window period of dry weather for haying was always a challenge. Wet, or even damp hay cannot be stored in a barn, as moisture in hay generates heat, and the results will be a roaring barn fire. One July afternoon and evening, all six of us raced against the clock as storm clouds loomed in the west. We risked losing a large part of our livestock food supply if the rain overtook us. As the final hay bale was thrown up on the last wagon load, we turned the tractor and wagon toward the barn. Just as the tractor and the wagon moved safely onto the barn floor, the clouds turned loose a torrent of rain. On our hike from the barn, our clothing was wet, but as we stood together in our kitchen near midnight, there was a sense of accomplishment. We had all worked at full speed to achieve a common goal of insuring that our horses and other livestock would have a winter supply of hay. By coming together as a team under adverse conditions, we had been successful.

I was in my early thirties when we moved to the Jamestown farm in western Ottawa County, Michigan, and I was not thinking about pheasant and rabbit hunting at the time. Growing up, except for my BB gun, there were few times when a firearm was on our premises. My mother was afraid of guns, and my dad had absolutely no interest in hunting.

On a couple of occasions, he had taken in guns as a trade-in on a piece of farm machinery. Specifically, I recall a nondescript rifle as a part of one of his barters.

"The rifling inside the gun barrel is not good," my dad had told me, "and it won't shoot straight."

With thoughts of owning my first deer rifle in mind, I procured a small amount of ammunition and set up a target. At thirty yards, the rifle sprayed bullets in various directions around the bullseye. My dad was right. The rifle was useless. Except for my BB gun, my military experience, and a day and a half hunting deer with a borrowed shotgun, I had not handled a firearm until after I was married.

Not long after our wedding, I had accepted an invitation to join my cousins, John, Ben, and Ken Miedema, to open the pheasant hunting season on their large southern Michigan farm. I was fascinated by the way their small spaniel located pheasants and then retrieved the downed birds to the hands of the hunters. Regarding my own success, however, I might as well have stayed home. Determined as I was, I was unable to hit a single bird that rose up before me. Meanwhile, my cousins never seemed to miss.

Although I was considerably embarrassed by my poor aim, I was, nevertheless, undaunted.

But now, it became very apparent that our newly purchased forty-one-acre farm, bordered by brushy gullies, was indeed a haven for wildlife, including pheasants. I might have an opportunity to redeem myself.

My firearm arsenal was comprised of a 30-30 bolt action rifle and a .410 single shot shotgun, both inappropriate for small game hunting. Gearing up for the approaching pheasant hunting season, I purchased a cheap single shot 12-gauge shotgun and a fifty dollar used J.C. Higgins (Sears & Roebuck) 12-gauge pump shotgun. Neither fit me very well. I was too naïve, however, to recognize the extent of the bad stock alignment in relation to my body build.

I went through nearly the entire pheasant hunting season before I finally brought down my first-ever pheasant. After so many failures, I'll long remember my excitement and sense of achievement upon bringing home that first trophy bird. The missed shots continued, however.

Finally, out of frustration, I decided on a new strategy. I would put my pump gun in storage and use only my single shot 12-gauge shotgun. Realizing I would have only one opportunity each time a pheasant went airborne, I needed to fully concentrate on the proper placement of that one shot. It worked.

Soon, I switched back to my pump gun. Using the same technique, I rarely missed flushing ringnecks for the duration of our stay on the farm. All through the fall of the year, our family chicken dinners were comprised mainly of the pheasants (wild chickens) raised on our own land.

Later, the glory days of Michigan pheasant hunting came to an end due to clean farming and housing developments. A person would be unlikely to find a single wild ringneck pheasant anywhere in its old habitat in southwestern Michigan.

No one in our family had ever been west of the Mississippi River, but a very good friend told about the wonders and beauty of the Wyoming and Montana areas. Marilyn and I could tell that our children were old enough to enjoy and appreciate such an endeavor. We pulled together enough funds and borrowed a tent. We would make this trip in our Volkswagen Beetle, pulling our fourteen-foot fishing boat. With six people in the VW, there was obviously no room for clothes and supplies. So, we carried those items in the boat.

We were traveling from our Ottawa County farm home well equipped with maps. But bad luck was soon to come our way.

We broke down in Dubuque, Iowa. We were fortunate, however, in being able to get our vehicle repaired and back on the road the same day. Traveling through Iowa, we were very much impressed with the beautiful, prosperous-looking farm buildings, along with the massive fields of corn. Because expressways were heavily used by truckers and by fast moving traffic, we decided to take rural side roads. That way we could better enjoy the natural beauty of the countryside. Furthermore, the towns through which we passed and often stopped were not tourist communities, and we experienced a warmth and friendliness unlike that of most tourist towns.

Crossing into South Dakota, extensive corn fields passed our car windows. But as we crossed the Missouri River in Central South Dakota, we witnessed an abrupt change in the terrain. We were now in ranch country.

Continuing westward through South Dakota, we came upon an attraction called Wall Drug. It turned out to be much more than a drug store. It was there that we had our first taste of buffalo burgers and

Looking across the South Dakota Badlands.
l to r: Dave, Bob, Marilyn, Jan and Nancy.

a chance to experience the well-known mechanical cowboy band. All that was required for that attraction were a few coins in the slot. Prior to strict highway billboard sign rules, Wall Drug signs were all over Michigan roadways, so we had heard about this tourist attraction long before we took our first trip. And, it was well worth the stop, as Wall

Drug offered a wide variety of souvenirs and entertainment for the entire family.

Just a few miles from Wall Drug, we came across the gateway to Badlands National Park. It was time to settle in for the night and we soon discovered a gem of a campground with only a handful of other campers. Hot and cold running water along with clean facilities all around added to the pleasure of a clear, beautiful "night to remember."

It was early June, ahead of the tourist rush, and it seemed as if we had the Badlands all to ourselves. Stopping to take photos and to climb the unique landforms of the Badlands was an unforgettable experience for our entire family and one of the highlights of our trip westward.

Taking in Mount Rushmore, we admired the likenesses of four of our greatest presidents—Washington, Jefferson, Lincoln, and Teddy Roosevelt.

Unwilling to devote more time to the South Dakota attractions, we bypassed Wind Cave and Custer State Park. These are places on the map that should not be missed, we understood, but we were eager to get to Yellowstone National Park and time was a factor. Driving north through the Black Hills, we understood how they got their name. The dark pine trees covering the sides of those enormous hills made the landscape appear black as coal. After passing Sturgis, we crossed into Wyoming just west of Spearfish, South Dakota.

Even though darkness had now set in, one could begin to grasp a sense of the openness and vastness of the area west of the Black Hills. Mile upon mile clicked across our odometer without seeing a sign of a living soul. Here and there, a yard light appeared far off in the distance, far away from the nearest neighbor or settlement of any kind. But after passing through Gillette, Wyoming, the land seemed uninhabited. Occasionally, we met another vehicle, usually a semi, but the lack of human habitation was striking, to say the least.

Eventually, the lights of a town appeared in the far distance, and we knew from studying our map that we were approaching Buffalo, Wyoming. It was too late to find a campground and set up our tent, so we decided to dip into our limited funds for a motel. We found one that had a vacancy, but with just one room available. That didn't stand in our way. We were a hardy bunch, each of us having grown up learning how to make do with whatever circumstances came our way. As long as there was a bathroom and running water, we were set to go. The next morning, as I stepped out the door, I was presented with a stunning, calendar-type view of the snowcapped Big Horn Mountains.

Although I had served an eighteen-month enlistment in the army, I had been stationed on the East Coast throughout my time in service. Other than in a photograph, no one in our family had ever seen a mountain.

Chugging our way up the Big Horn Mountains, we encountered breathtaking gorges and steep climbs, which took a toll on our VW Bug. Reaching the town of Ten Sleep, we experienced a sample of the local culture.

Searching for water for our thirsty VW Bug, we were told to check to see if the local bar could supply us. It was 10:00 a.m. on a weekday, and the place was jumping. There were people everywhere and the jukebox seemed at full volume.

A friendly bar occupant with a water jug accompanied us to our vehicle and we were soon on our way to Yellowstone National Park. I soon came to realize that we were in ranch country, and unlike farmers, ranchers do not have much to do when not working cattle. Mornings in the local tavern provide a social setting.

Winding our way up the mountains toward Yellowstone Park, our VW Bug had all it could do to negotiate the steeper climbs. Wherever there were passing lanes, vehicles passed us in droves. Eventually, we arrived at the main Yellowstone Campground near Old Faithful Geyser, and we pitched our tent in the snow. We did as other campers and ate our evening meal. But there was a bear in camp.

Soon, he jumped on the supper table of a nearby man and woman. They didn't see the bear coming, and when he landed on the table, they broke speed records vacating the dinner table.

The Volkswagen trunk was open, and a large watermelon had been left in it. The bear was heading for the car trunk. I told Marilyn, "Let the bear have the melon."

"No," she exclaimed, and headed for the melon.

I expected a catastrophe, but Marilyn beat the bear to the VW, grabbed the melon, and raced with it back to the tent. The bear would have to wait.

On our way home from Yellowstone, we stopped to fish the Oahe Reservoir in South Dakota, where we caught some nice walleyes and a fish we had never before seen—a sauger, which looked like a cross between a walleye and a perch.

Shortly after returning from our Yellowstone trip, I changed jobs and went to work for D.C. Heath Publishing Company.

Our Yellowstone adventure had been such a pleasurable experience for our family that we decided to take another westward journey, with Glacier National Park as our destination. After a two-year wait, I borrowed three hundred dollars from the local bank and built a cartop boat rack from two-by-four lumber and discarded inner tubes. Loading our fourteen-foot aluminum boat atop our vehicle, we put the boat motor in the trunk of the new Plymouth, packed our recently purchased family tent, extra clothes, sleeping bags, and fishing rods in the trunk, and hired a neighbor farm boy to look after our livestock. We were fortunate from the standpoint that the publisher for whom I worked allowed employees to use company cars for personal use. Nevertheless, I notified my employer of our plans and received approval.

Driving north to Ludington, we boarded the Lake Michigan ferry to Manitowoc, Wisconsin. Leaving Manitowoc, we began camping our way westward. And soon we were again crossing the Missouri River into ranch country. As the afternoon waned, we began to look for a suitable camping location. Unexpectedly, we came upon a campground on a small, treeless lake. We soon discovered that the campground rented out paddle boats. Marilyn and the family spent the rest of the day paddling around the lake, enjoying the beautiful weather and the ranch country atmosphere.

Tent camping our way westward. **l to r:** *Nancy, Marilyn, and Dave.*

We then revisited Wall Drug and the Badlands before heading north into Montana. Driving through eastern Montana to Billings, we dropped in to see Marilyn's cousin and her family. Without a means of communication, we were unable to notify them in advance. Nevertheless, they were very gracious, and we shared a delicious brunch.

Turning south at Livingston, Montana, along the Yellowstone River, we discovered a place called Pine Creek, comprised only of a store-gas station combination, along with a set of cabins. Night after night along our route we had been putting up our tent, and the thought of a night in a cabin sounded inviting. The price was six dollars a night. We ended up staying several nights and used it as a base of operation. We could not have made a better decision.

Before leaving our Michigan farm home, I had read in a national outdoor magazine about a fishing expert who owned a sporting goods store in Livingston. We decided to visit his store to see if he would direct us to an area lake where we might catch some fish. After a friendly visit, he advised us to try our luck at a nearby lake. He also gave us directions as to its location. After purchasing fishing licenses and night crawlers for bait, Dave, Bob, and I gathered our fishing tackle and followed a two-track road through ranch land, between snowcapped mountain ranges.

After driving several miles, we came upon a body of water and took note of a dilapidated, unstable fifteen-foot dock. There was not a boat on the lake, and there was not a human in sight.

Launching our fourteen-foot aluminum rowboat with its five horsepower motor, we let out our lines with crawler harnesses attached. To our delight, rainbow trout almost immediately began hitting our bait. One after another, Dave, Bob, and I were fighting twelve- to fifteen-inch trout into the boat. It was a scenario that fishermen see in their dreams.

With our limit in our cooler, we returned to our cabin for a delicious, fresh-caught rainbow trout dinner, and with plans for another fishing adventure the next day.

Returning to Daily Lake as planned, I soon put my fishing rod aside, as Dave and Bob were landing trout one after another, and I was busy keeping lines untangled, putting bait on hooks and fish in the cooler. Adventures like this are rare, and I was glad I could share it with my two sons.

Headquarters of a large ranch were located directly across the road from our cabin, and son Bob was invited to help with the branding of young cattle. It was a unique experience for him, and a process usually seen only in the movies.

While staying in our cabin in the aptly named Paradise Valley, we were informed about a rather "blue collar" resort nearby where swimming was available. To our delight, we discovered an open-air pool containing warm water flowing down from a mountain. As we arrived, only three or four others were enjoying the pool. As far as Marilyn was concerned, an afternoon of swimming at Chico Hot Springs was a highlight of that trip.

Near Chico Hot Springs, we came across an obviously seldom-used two-track road that meandered up a mountainside. Out of curiosity, we decided to proceed up the road to see where it might lead. After some crooks and turns on our upward journey, we came to a sizeable boulder directly in the road. Apparently, the road had been unused for a considerable time, which only added to the mystery of the situation. After debating our next move, Bob and Dave volunteered to try moving the boulder.

Dave and Bob remove a boulder from the road on our way to a ghost town.

Return to Farm Life and Vacation Adventures

With all the strength at their command, they were able to roll the large stone out of our way, and we continued up the mountain. Suddenly, we found ourselves rolling into a completely deserted ghost town. Buildings were well preserved, and we took note of a large wooden wheel above a small stream. We wondered if this might be a former gold mining operation.

Pocket gophers are a nemesis to Montana ranchers. These pests are destructive to alfalfa fields and pastureland. We had learned about these rodents before leaving on our journey. We had decided to bring two .22-caliber rifles with us, for the possibility of some long-range shooting. While staying in our cabin at Pine Creek, we decided to seek out ranchland where we might use our .22s.

Dave (left) and Bob, take aim at pocket gophers north of Yellowstone National Park.

Driving on a gravel road just north of Yellowstone National Park, Dave, Bob, and I scanned the vast ranchland for a sign of pocket gophers. After several miles, we spotted a colony of gophers on a hillside. A rancher was sitting on his tractor nearby. As long as we were careful not to shoot any livestock, he was glad to give us permission to rid his land of the varmints that were tearing up his pastureland. We spent a good part of that afternoon plinking away with our .22s.

While the boys and I were out and about, Marilyn enjoyed a couple of leisurely afternoons relaxing and reading back at the cabin, while the girls played around the cabin and raced pine cones down a nearby creek.

Our stay at Pine Creek had been memorable, but our itinerary called for new adventures, and we pointed our red Plymouth toward the northwest. It was early June, before the tourist season. At one point, we pulled over to the side of the road to watch a herd of antelope trot across the landscape. As we stood beside our vehicle, we took note of the absolute silence.

We didn't know what to expect when we arrived at Lewis & Clark Caverns. None of us had ever visited a cave, and since it was in a state park, the cavern was not heavily advertised. We bought our tickets and were soon riding a cable car up the side of a mountain.

Entering the mouth of the cave, we soon came upon a room full of stalagmites and stalactites. A park ranger was on hand and gave an entertaining presentation.

Then we were on our way to Glacier National Park. We would need to camp one more night, however, before reaching our destination. Previous research had indicated a KOA Campground on our route.

Pulling into the campground, we found only one other camper and those folks were in a small motor home. We set up our tent and threw down sleeping bags. There was not much sleep for me, however.

To my dismay, I had learned that the campground had an absentee owner. In case of problems, there was little recourse. We were in a wilderness area just south of Glacier National Park—grizzly country. I did not inform the family. Early the next morning, we hurriedly packed our gear and tent and were on our way to the park.

Vehicles traveling northward through Glacier National Park are on the outside lane all the way through the park. There are hairpin turns throughout, and there are no guardrails. A friend who had driven the route earlier had told me, "The going to the sun road through Glacier is not for the faint of heart." He was not exaggerating.

The views in Glacier National Park are nothing short of spectacular. We came upon beautiful waterfalls, and mountain goats clung to the very face of mountainsides.

As we were leaving Glacier National Park, one of our daughters began to experience a bit of queasiness. We did not want to be on the road with a sick family member, so, we decided to hastily head back to our farm home. Driving into the night, we came to Roosevelt National Memorial Badlands where we threw down sleeping bags and slept under the stars. Early the next morning, we tossed sleeping bags into our vehicle, and concentrating on our destination, we were soon pulling into our farmyard.

We pull into our farm driveway after our second trip to the west.

We had taken many photos along the way, and we had them made into slides. Later, many evenings were taken up entertaining extended family members with our slide projector and reliving those adventurous days.

During most of the years we occupied the Jamestown farm, a feral Maltese cat lived in our barn. She was a beautiful animal but was extremely secretive and rarely seen. Dogs were always a part of our farm landscape, however, and they all free ranged. Allowing farm dogs and cats to run loose was a common practice at that time. All pets were brought into the house at night, however.

Small animal pets included our beagle, "Freckles," our bird hunting dog, "Dutchie," a most affectionate German shorthair, and Marilyn's dog, "Polly," a purebred English shepherd.

The Jamestown farm location provided many recreational outlets for the children. Even though saddles were available, they usually rode bareback. They all became very good riders and, fortunately, there was never an accident involving one of the kids and a horse.

In order to earn money in the summer, they sometimes picked pickles for twenty-five cents a bucket at a nearby farm.

In the winter, the steep hill beside our house was used for sledding and for toboggan runs. Homework and farm chores took up much of the after-school time in the winter and gathering around the television set was a regular nightly event.

Our daughters played outside whenever weather permitted and sometimes played among the pawpaw patches that clung to the nearby steep hillsides.

Some summer days were spent playing in a treehouse I had built directly behind our farmhouse. Perhaps motivated by seeing me typing freelance stories for newspapers and magazines, our kids started their own play newspaper based in the treehouse. Oldest son, Dave, was the editor-in-chief. They titled their newspaper the *Hadbaw Star*, the initials of which, according to them, stood for "High and Dry But All Wet." Their newspaper was not widely circulated.

Dave and Bob played Little League baseball and I resumed playing fast-pitch softball as a part of a team sponsored by a church we were attending at the time. At first, having been away from the game for several years, my timing was off. The team manager used me as a substitute, but after a couple games, I went in as a pinch hitter and lined the ball over the fence. From that point forward, I served as the catcher and clean-up hitter.

The family nearly always accompanied me to my softball games, and the ballpark served as a social setting with bleachers and a concession stand.

From time to time, I ventured south to the Allegan State Forest for hunting and fishing opportunities, and one summer evening there was an occurrence that could very well have ended in unspeakable tragedy.

It took place on a Sunday evening when daughter Jan had accompanied me on a trout fishing venture. We had driven to a trout stream in Allegan County, south of our Jamestown farm home. We had not had any luck fishing. As daylight faded, we returned to our vehicle.

To our dismay, our car refused to start. I tried numerous remedies but had no success. This was before the advent of cell phones, and we were without means of communication. Furthermore, we were in a state forest where there was little traffic. Eventually, I heard the sound of an approaching vehicle. I waved my arms, and the driver stopped.

I told the driver of our plight, asked him to call our home phone, and gave him the number. It would be a long-distance call with a fee. We had no idea as to whether he would follow through.

Meanwhile, brother Harold, his wife, Abbey, and son, Doug, had unexpectedly stopped at our farm home and were there when the call came in. Harold told Marilyn that he would rescue us.

About an hour later, brother Harold pulled up to greet us. He had brought along his son, Doug, and our two sons, Dave and Bob. Our roadside visitor had been a good Samaritan. We hopped into Harold's station wagon and headed for our home. We were about ten miles from our farm when suddenly, out of nowhere, there was a flash of lights. With lightning speed, a thought flashed across my mind, "We won't get out of this alive."

A vehicle with a carload of people had run through a stop sign at fifty-five miles per hour and hit us broadside.

The impact of the crash threw me, with tremendous force, against the side of my older brother, Harold, who was behind the steering wheel. Our station wagon skidded sideways, rolled on its side, then on its top.

Suffering severe pain from broken ribs, Harold crawled out through the broken window on his side. I crawled out the opposite window. Harold's young son, Doug, was lying unconscious near the roof of our upside-down vehicle. Crawling on hands and knees to his motionless son, I heard Harold breathlessly exclaim, "I think he's dead."

Besides Doug, our son Bob and daughter Jan were thrown from our vehicle. They landed in the middle of the blacktop road. Dave was not thrown from the vehicle. This was before seatbelts were used in cars and trucks.

Because of the large number of people involved, Jan was compelled to ride in the front of the ambulance while enduring severe pain. X-rays at the hospital revealed that she had broken ribs, two broken collarbones, and two leg fractures. The emergency staff had misread the situation.

Jan spent time in the hospital, and Harold suffered lingering effects from severely broken ribs. Miraculously, however, there were no fatalities resulting from this nightmarish accident.

Throughout my earlier years, I had been involved in music to a large extent. My parents were choir singers, and my older brothers had sung and played instruments throughout high school. During our stay at Jamestown, my two older brothers moved with their families to the Grand Rapids area, a few miles from our farm. We soon formed a southern gospel quartet which included brothers Harold and Don, Don's son-in-law, Jim, with Don's daughter Sandy Veldheer on piano. We sang southern gospel in churches throughout southwestern Michigan and sometimes live on area radio stations.

Meanwhile, with our children becoming more independent, Marilyn began taking a few college classes in order to qualify for substitute teaching. Soon, she was substitute teaching in area schools and contributing significantly to our family income.

As a publisher's representative selling textbooks to schools, I was in a line of work that was in considerable turmoil. Textbook companies were merging one after the other and being bought out by firms with no experience in the textbook field. Continual management changes added to our chaotic working conditions. At one point, I left the publishing field and operated a reading clinic.

In order to supplement our family income, I briefly taught night school classes in the Grand Rapids Public Schools Adult Education Program. I also wrote a weekly outdoor column for a daily and several weekly newspapers.

Much of our life at the Jamestown farm revolved around our children. As parents, we never knew, as a certainty, what incident might be just around the corner. As parents, we came to realize, however, that whenever there are four active and alert children around, there will always be someone who insists on keeping the record straight. One day, our teenage and preteen children were temporarily left home while Marilyn and I tended to an errand. When we returned, one of our offspring spoke up. "Mom—while you and Dad were away, Bob rode the

*A family gathering at the home of Harold and Abbey Sprik in Hudsonville, Michigan. **l to r:** Margaret, Reg, Edna, Abbey, Harold, Jim Veldheer, Sandy Veldheer and Marilyn. Photographer: Don.*

Shetland pony through the house."

The question then arises as to our reasons for leaving our Ottawa County farm and moving to Bellaire, after so many wonderful family experiences at that location. A main reason was the encroachment of the city. New houses were being built at a rapid rate on nearby property, changing the area into suburban USA. I did not want to be swallowed up in that movement.

Furthermore, residents of the area were primarily of the same Dutch ethnic lifestyle. Religious rule prevailed. All businesses were closed on Sundays. Children were not allowed to play outdoors on Sundays. Attendance at movies and dances was strictly forbidden for adults as well as for younger people. Hunting, fishing, swimming, and all other outdoor activities were strictly forbidden on Sundays. I was concerned about the concepts our children might absorb from continuing to live in that type of ethnic environment. Although I was of the same heritage as the people around us, I had grown up in communities with people of various economic and cultural lifestyles. I wanted our children to experience a much broader diversification in regard to school and social life in general.

Each year, our oldest son and oldest daughter brought home the vast majority of the blue ribbons from school system-wide field day events involving running and jumping activities. Yet, our oldest son was being denied participation in sports at the high school level. Regardless of her superior athletic ability, our oldest daughter was not allowed to participate in cheerleading. As a former college football player and head coach at the high school level, I could evaluate athletic talent accurately, and I came to realize that name recognition and politics were strongly in play. Our sons and daughters would probably never have an equal opportunity. As a caring parent, I was not going to allow this to happen. It was time to move.

- Chapter Ten -
Bellaire and Retirement Travels

It was the summer of 1969, and we were determined to relocate before the start of the 1969–70 school year. We had visited several Antrim County towns and villages, Bellaire among them.

Through research, we learned that the Bellaire School System provided full academic and athletic programs. The village itself was a town of only a thousand residents, nearly the exact number of people living in the community where I went to high school.

The village of Bellaire hosted churches of various denominations (indicating a culturally diverse citizenry), local industries that provided very good incomes for local families, and a grocery store in a downtown building.

Furthermore, there were two medical offices and a dental office for health care needs. Walking along Main Street, in addition to shopping in a clothing store and hardware store, a person could enjoy a meal in a very fine restaurant or take in a movie at the well-furnished theatre. To add to the attractiveness of the village, a river ran through the center of the town and it was the county seat. Since we were free to move to any location we so desired, Bellaire was a logical choice. The move to the location of our choosing did not come about without abundant challenges, however.

We had borrowed money from an Ottawa County bank near our Jamestown home in order to make substantial improvements to our farmhouse and barn. The auction sale we had arranged in order to dispose of our farm machinery and other items was poorly attended and did not produce the revenue we had expected. After paying off our bank loan, there was not much money remaining from the sale to help with our move.

There was a shortage of three-bedroom rental houses in Bellaire, so we arranged to rent a cottage in Elk Rapids while we continued to look for suitable housing. A gracious farmer outside of Elk Rapids volunteered to temporarily board our horses at no charge. While staying in the Elk Rapids cottage, we continued to seek housing in Bellaire. Eventually, a house immediately north of Bellaire became available and we made arrangements to rent it. Pastureland, suitable for our horses, was connected to the property. It was July of 1969.

We immediately moved our belongings to our new Bellaire location, and the younger family members rode the horses over the estimated twenty-five miles of roads and bridges to our new Bellaire location.

Storm clouds were forming in the textbook publishing industry, however. Small publishers, many of which had been producing textbooks for decades, were being bought out by large conglomerates and management changes were taking place at a whirlwind pace. Relationships between management and field representatives became highly impersonal. Shortly after our move to Bellaire, I was caught up in it.

Prior to our Bellaire relocation, I had received approval to move to any area within the boundaries of my territory. Shortly after settling into our rental home, however, new company management insisted I move back downstate to be centrally located in my territory. I refused. I was immediately terminated.

The company car, which we had been allowed to use for our personal vehicle, was taken back by the publisher. Marilyn did not yet have her degree and was unemployable. I had no choice other than to work at a local resort for low wages. We fell behind on our bills. Creditors came after us with "fangs." Our electricity was shut off.

Over a period of time, however, and by means of student loans, I had renewed my teacher certification. I accepted a modestly paying teaching position at a nearby school system where I taught for two

We celebrate Marilyn's graduation from Western Michigan University.

years. In the meantime, Marilyn earned her BA degree plus her teaching certification and had signed a teaching contract. Slowly, we began to climb out of the financial hole.

Overall, it was a bright and shining renewal for our family. Our daughters and sons meshed well into the new school system and our entire family was warmly welcomed into the community. I was elected president of the Athletic Boosters. Marilyn and I were delighted to observe the younger members of our family having an opportunity to participate and even excel in athletics and other activities.

Oldest son, Dave, dominated in the Bellaire football program, and went on to all-state honors. Jan and Nancy became cheerleaders, and Nancy served as a class officer throughout junior high and high school. Jan joined the high school ski team. She demonstrated her athletic ability in track and field by running in the Michigan State Track Finals and by setting the Bellaire high jump record, which she held for twenty years.

Dave became a star player in the Chain of Lakes softball league, which was comprised of some of the best athletes in northwestern Lower Michigan. Year after year, he led the league in home runs, as an outfielder and first baseman.

In basketball, Dave became an all-stater, leading the Bellaire team with a twenty point per game average and a berth in the state regional finals. Competing in the Class D State Track and Field Championships, Dave came away with the silver medal in the high jump, clearing the bar somewhere above the six-foot mark.

Dave went on to play four years as a star tight end at Michigan Technological University (better known as "Michigan Tech"). His athletic scholarship paid most of his college expenses. Our family enjoyed many weekends watching Dave compete. On one such occasion, Dave scored the team's only touchdown, as his team went on to defeat its opponent by a score of six to zero.

Instead of going on to college, Bob joined the United States Navy. Serving on the USS *Hancock*, Bob helped with the evacuation of Vietnamese refugees near the end of the Vietnam War.

Jan attended Northern Michigan University for two years and completed requirements for her bachelor of arts degree at Spring Arbor University.

Nancy attended Alma College for one year before transferring to Northwestern Michigan College for a degree in applied science.

Shortly after our move to Bellaire, a set of circumstances came about that heavily influenced our life in our new community. Doug Watrous, a senior at Bellaire High School, moved in with us. Doug had grown up fishing and hunting in and around Bellaire. With Doug as our guide, we learned about local fishing and hunting opportunities in the area.

Unlike our previous Jamestown location, where rivers and lakes were unfishable due to human and agricultural pollution, Bellaire area

l to r: Doug Watrous and Ron Klintworth join me in a search for perch.

lakes and streams were quite free of pollutants. The nearby Jordan River flowed clear and pristine and was soon to be designated a Natural River. This stream is now recommended for classification as a Wild and Scenic River.

One evening, Doug guided me to a rarely fished tributary of the Jordan River. Over the following years, when I sought an afternoon of solitude, this small stream often became my destination. Scrambling through thick brush and over logs, I could usually locate a couple brown or rainbow trout to make a delicious evening meal. Throughout the years that I fished that stream, there was only one occasion when I met another fisherman. When that happened, I packed up my rod and reel and departed for my vehicle. It was as if my privacy had been invaded.

Intermediate Lake became the site for most of my ice fishing, although I caught some nice fish on Lake Bellaire. Walleyes were nearly always the sought-after fish, as they provided excellent table fare. Most of us used tip-ups, with minnows for bait. On one occasion, Doug and I left tip-ups out overnight, a common practice at that time. At daylight, we found two tip-ups with flags flying.

Reeling in our lines, we brought through the ice a six-pound pike and a five-pound walleye. Not bad, considering the fact that Doug and I were asleep while this was going on. Shortly thereafter, the Michigan Department of Natural Resources put an end to this type of overnight fishing, and countless anglers lost bundles of tip-ups to eager conservation officers equipped with night vision and binoculars. As is true with the population in general, there are fishermen who demonstrate a lack of awareness, such as those caught fishing without a license. I have never known of one so brainless, however, as to request the return of his or her confiscated tip-ups.

Among cherished memories are fishing trips to Ontario, Canada. Doug and son-in-law Bill Bock were often included in these camping and fishing excursions. The walleyes we caught provided most of our nutrition on these ventures.

One memorable trip included Marilyn, along with daughters Jan and Nancy. Each daughter brought a friend for companionship, while Doug Watrous and I served as guides. Our fourteen-foot aluminum rowboat towed a canoe up and over logs and rapids to our campsite on an oversized boulder on a river bend. Fish were not biting, but, nevertheless, our seven-member party enjoyed a memorable true wilderness camping adventure.

Unaccustomed to handling fishing equipment, one of our daughter's friends accidently tossed her entire fishing rod and reel into a pool along the river. Fortunately, we were able to drag a hook through the pool and retrieve the fishing gear.

Meanwhile, the girls discovered a pool fed by the river and located directly upstream and out of sight of our campsite. The girls ventured over to the backwater for a cooling dip.

Jan's school friend, Sue, was an early riser. As I started the morning cooking fire and the coffeepot, Sue and I sat across from each other, absorbing the rising of the sun and the absolute silence of the wilderness surroundings. The soul thirsts for such moments.

Prior to our move to Bellaire, we had invested substantial funds into improvements to our Jamestown farmhouse. Brand new aluminum siding had been applied to the exterior and a new oil furnace replaced the original coal-burning furnace. Considerable improvements had also been made on the barn. Marilyn's reaction to moving from our upgraded farmhouse was mixed. "Now that the house is fixed up, we're going to move?" At the same time, Marilyn shared my frustration regarding our sons' and daughters' lack of opportunities in our Jamestown location. Prior to moving to Bellaire, I had promised Marilyn that I would build a new house in our new location. But it wasn't that easy.

Shortly after moving to our Bellaire rental house, we began looking for property on which to build. There would need to be facilities for our three horses, which meant a sizeable piece of land, at least ten acres. And through word of mouth, we found what we thought we were seeking, a ten-acre chunk of land not far from beautiful Torch Lake. We put down a five hundred dollar deposit. As time went on, however, we became more and more uncomfortable with the location.

Several houses were in close proximity and the property was near a busy county highway. If the horses escaped their enclosure, they could create problems with neighbors. Worse, one or more could be struck by a vehicle, particularly if they broke free at night when it would be difficult for motorists to see them. Our increasing anxiety over the possible problems finally brought us to the home of the landowners with a request to back out of the deal.

The landowners were exceedingly gracious, and very willingly arranged paperwork to reverse the purchase. Not only that, but they insisted on returning our five-hundred-dollar deposit, even though we had offered to forfeit the down payment. But serendipity was about to come our way.

In order to take advantage of the recreational offerings in our new geographic location, Marilyn and I each bought snowshoes. Doug Watrous was living with us at the time, and he suggested a snowshoe hike through a rural area just east of Bellaire.

As we ascended the top of a hill, a beautiful landscape in all directions came into view. I remembered seeing an old battered real estate sign at the foot of the hill. Immediately, Marilyn and I began discussing the possibility of purchasing the property. We did not know if the property had already been sold and if the old real estate sign was nothing more than a relic of the past. Nevertheless, we did some research and learned that the twenty-acre piece of land was available for purchase. We made an offer, and it was accepted. Now, we needed to figure out how to get the house built, and a new acquaintance gave us an idea.

Doug in the snowshoes he wore to help us find the building site for the Bellaire house.

Soon, in response to our telephone call, a representative from Wisconsin-based firm Capp Homes appeared at our door. He left a colored catalog showing various types of homes available through their company, along with a number of floor plans. He also told us all materials for the home would be cut to proper length and would be dropped off at our building site. He highly recommended a three-foot overhang on the roof. Although the necessary paperwork involved created considerable frustration, we looked upon the building of our dream home as a journey, an adventure. We would build it ourselves, stick by stick. One day in May 1972, returning home from my teaching position, I stopped to check our newly purchased property. Capp Homes had made their delivery.

Even though the materials were of the highest quality, various pieces of lumber and plywood were strewn topsy-turvy in several piles. Nothing was labeled, and lumber was not cut to proper length, as had been promised. Considering the fact that I had never built as much as a birdhouse, I now fully realized the difficult task before us. I was undeterred, however.

It was June of 1972 and the heat of the day-after-day boiling sun was near record-breaking. The basement had been dug, and sons Dave and Bob, along with Doug Watrous and me, began digging the footings through rock-hard clay. Because the house had a walk-out basement, there were various levels of footings. We needed to be as exact as possible. Using pickaxes and round-nosed shovels, we completed the ground work.

One look at the blockwork and it was readily apparent that the work was done by first timers. The rows were somewhat uneven, but we made it all come out level at the top. The blocks would later be covered by stucco anyway, and no one would know the difference. Actually, the stucco was applied many years later when the house was repainted.

Although I had never read a blueprint, I had one advantage. A segment of my industrial arts class in middle school was devoted to mechanical drawing and I found the coursework very interesting and easy to learn. Furthermore, as mentioned earlier, I had experienced the benefits of an excellent high school geometry teacher. That small amount of knowledge transferred over to interpretation of the blue-prints for the house. Step by step, Dave, Bob, Doug, and I installed the framing for the entire house. A neighbor, experienced with building, was hired to help with the rafters, and I put on the roof boards.

A nearby roofer was hired to install the asphalt roof. Brief consultations with a heating contractor and with a person experienced with plumbing were all that was needed for me to make sure we had water and heat. With considerable interior work remaining, we prepared to leave our rented house and move to our new home. But a large obstacle remained.

Front view of the Bellaire home we built from the ground up.

The well drilling company we hired could not find water at the chosen site behind the house. Finally, at a depth of two hundred feet, a small vein of water was probed. But it was in blue clay, and the water quality was very poor. We decided to look elsewhere on the property. A local teacher who could "water witch" came out to help. After water witching a number of locations around the periphery of the house, it was decided to drill in a lower elevation about one hundred yards from the house. Returning from my teaching job the next afternoon, I quickly learned that a large water vein had been struck in a layer of gravel ninety feet below the surface. In short order, water pipe was extended to our house and connected to our water pump. Our huge concern over the possibility of a lack of water supply was now behind us.

Building our house from the ground up was not a matter of choice. We simply did not have the financial resources to hire much help. Doug Watrous lived with us and worked for meager wages. A neighbor, who had recently built his own house, showed me how to "sweat" the joints of the copper plumbing. A heating contractor, who had recently moved to the area, very graciously showed me how to install the heating system. Neither would accept any payment for their services.

In June of 1973, our house reached the point where we could move in. I had tried to be meticulous about the plumbing installation. Immediately after moving, we were in for a surprise, however.

"Turn off the water," I yelled to Marilyn from the lower level of the house. Water was spraying all over the basement. I had missed the soldering of a couple copper joints. Fortunately, I was able to dry up the pipes and make corrections. Except for new sink fixtures put in later, the plumbing I originally installed still functions properly forty-eight years later.

Capp Homes provided top-quality building materials. Cupboards, doors, and all trim are made from oak. The three-foot soffit overhang recommended by the Capp representative has eliminated considerable weather damage to windows, doors, and siding as well as providing

A swimming pool enjoyed by kids and grandkids at our Bellaire home.

shade from the hot sun. Doug Watrous's dad, Bob, constructed split-stone fireplaces for our living room and downstairs family room.

As time went on, a large, above-ground swimming pool was purchased and provided a cooling summer dip, as well as much enjoyment for our visiting grandkids. From free materials, Marilyn and I built a fire-pit that, along with a freezer for homemade ice cream, has served as a gathering place for our expanded family.

Shortly after arriving in Bellaire, we learned about girls' AAU track meets being held at various locations in Michigan. These were summertime events. Doug Watrous agreed to help coach such a team in Bellaire, and soon a group of young girls was formed into a team. Practices were held on a makeshift track behind the local school (all grades were then in one building), and meets were scheduled throughout the state.

Jan and Nancy were eager participants. Later, and as an adult, a woman who had participated in our AAU events told us that the medals and ribbons she won at these meets had greatly benefited her self-image.

In the spring of 1970, Bellaire school administrators decided to bring baseball back into the school athletic program. Learning of my background as a teacher and coach, the athletic director asked me to take over the program as head coach. New uniforms were ordered and games were scheduled.

At first, our baseball team had difficulty competing, and we suffered several losses to experienced teams. It was a period of time, however, when Bellaire High School benefited from an accumulation of outstanding athletes. As the season rolled on, that talent began to reveal itself, and the Bellaire team began to beat teams that had defeated us earlier in the season.

Because of a contract dispute, my baseball coaching career at Bellaire ended after one season. Later, while teaching in a neighboring school system, I was asked to take over as coach of that varsity basketball team. I declined the offer, however, as I was in the midst of building our new Bellaire home.

In order to keep ourselves physically fit after moving to Bellaire, Marilyn and I decided to join the rapidly expanding running community. After considerable training, we reached a point where we could run three miles without needing to walk. We began to enter road races, and to our delight, we sometimes even won an age group medal. In the meantime, however, our lives were darkened by the loss of our two-year-old grandson.

In order to memorialize the child of daughter Jan

One of our many 5K road races.

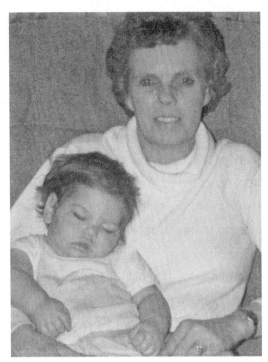

One of her favorite things. Marilyn cradles sleeping grandson, Brian, in her arms.

and her husband, Bill, we organized the Brian Bock Memorial Run. We made arrangements with the Bellaire village for the use of Craven Park for race headquarters and laid out a 5K course. We added a one-mile fun walk/run for those not up to the 5K (three mile) distance.

The Brian Bock Memorial Run carried on for three years with about one hundred participants for each event. Jan and Bill donated the race proceeds to Munson Hospital Pediatrics.

Marilyn and I continued entering road races throughout northwestern Michigan, the Upper Peninsula, and Ontario, Canada. Of all the races we entered, there is one that stands out in my mind. That is not because I performed so well. Rather, it was because of the stifling heat.

Marilyn usually entered races with me, but in this case, and in the hour prior to the start, she very wisely declined to enter. The event was a 10K race (more than six miles) through woodlands, on two-track roads with no shade. The 10:00 a.m. starting time was far too late to begin a summertime six-mile road race.

After about two miles into the race, I pulled off my T-shirt and tossed it to the side of the two-track. But, the heat from the blazing sun was unrelenting. About one-half mile before the finish, I experienced something new. I felt a minor burning sensation each time one of my arms swung past my side.

Shortly after crossing the finish line, along with a group of running friends, we drove to the waterfront. After hurriedly removing running shoes, we plunged into the cooling waters of the nearby harbor. There has never been a time before or since that occasion when cooling lake water has been as utterly refreshing.

In a variety of ways, modern farming methods had nearly wiped out the pheasant population in southern Michigan. These game birds were still plentiful in parts of South Dakota, however, and a remnant population remained in south central Michigan.

Over a period of years, I had lost all interest in deer hunting. Although Marilyn and some of our young family members liked it, I never had a taste for venison. Pheasants and ruffed grouse (pats) have provided our family with delicious table fare, however.

A friend, Phil Reed, had family in the Hillsdale area who owned farmland. Phil invited me to his family farm on several occasions where we could flush a few game birds. Son-in-law Bill sometimes went with me. But, after moving to Bellaire, most of my pheasant hunting was done in South Dakota. Bill Bock often accompanied me.

Roaming South Dakota game production areas and roadside ditches with our hunting dogs, Bill and I enjoyed some delightful bird hunting experiences. Several years later, I met with Jim Veldheer, who has since passed away, for nearly a week of hunting South Dakota prairies. Jim was a landowner near the town of Platte. There, we could step out his door and view the Missouri River Breaks. Although I have been considered to be reasonably accurate with my 12-gauge Winchester shotgun, filling my game bag has never been my purpose afield. It has always been about my hunting dog, the beauty of the surroundings, and the companionship of people who are important in my life. That, and the pos-

Two canine friends help me bring down a limit of South Dakota pheasants.

sibility that my efforts might produce, at least, a modicum of success. But, of all my hunting experiences, there is one particular occasion that stands out because of its uniqueness.

It was in the midst of the spring turkey hunting season and I had not met with success. For some odd reason, I had returned home in the late afternoon, and to my surprise, the vehicle belonging to my brother Don and wife, Edna, sat in our driveway.

After customary greetings, I invited Don to join me to look for turkeys in nearby fields. Don hopped into my vehicle, and about a mile and a half from our home, we saw turkeys cross the road. Some were bearded (male birds and a legal target).

Hoping for a shot at one of the birds, and so that I could not be accused of shooting from my vehicle, I hastily backed my car up the hill. A fire lane was nearby and I quickly loaded my shotgun, ran down the hill, and waited. Suddenly, racing birds appeared and I touched off a shot. The turkeys were moving so fast that I hit the bearded bird behind the one I shot at. Sometimes, good luck beats accuracy.

Don was hugely impressed. Although he used to enjoy hunting, he had long since given it up. Returning home, Don helped me collect a supply of hot water in a large container. "We need to get the feathers off this bird and get it dressed out right away," he exclaimed.

Brother Don joins me to show the wild turkey we brought home.

The nicely cleaned turkey was put to rest in our freezer. A few months later, Don called and asked if they could again stop in for a short visit. As the centerpiece of our evening dinner, Marilyn provided this same roasted wild turkey.

"You shouldn't be eating so much," we heard Edna tell Don.

His answer was brief, "This is the best turkey I've ever had."

One by one, each of our children went her and his own way. Bob had enlisted for three years in the US Navy. The others were off to college or were married and holding down jobs. Their horses still roamed the pasture, however. One day, Marilyn and I discussed the idea of saddling up the horses and going for a horseback ride. Marilyn was somewhat hesitant but decided to go along with the idea.

During that one summer, we rode the horses along rural roads and two-tracks. One very pleasant afternoon, we rode several miles to the home of our daughter Jan. After returning from that jaunt, however, a foreboding thought crossed my mind.

"If a wild bird or animal suddenly jumps up before the horses, our mounts might rise up on hind legs and throw us off," I said to Marilyn.

Even worse, we reasoned, if a horse fell on either of us in that type of scenario, one of us could be crippled up for life and ruin the remainder of our retirement. Subsequently, the saddles and bridles were put away where they remain to this day.

To a large extent, our family has been education minded. After raising a family, Marilyn earned her bachelor of arts degree from Western Michigan University. Dave graduated with a bachelor of science degree from Michigan Tech University, and Jan received her bachelor of arts degree from Spring Arbor University. Nancy graduated with an associate's degree from Northwestern Michigan College, and I received a bachelor of science degree from Western Michigan University.

Continuing with my formal education, I earned a master of arts degree from Central Michigan University. I later learned that my master's thesis was being used as a research document in the university library. This was somewhat astonishing, since earlier in my life, frustrated and aggravated teachers plus a top school administrator had, in a sense, voted me "Most Likely Not To Succeed."

It was largely a matter of economics. I had turned down the offer of a teaching position in order to start a business selling library books to schools. I had worked for nearly fifteen years as a textbook representative, so I knew the administrators in most of the northern Michigan schools. However, I soon learned that library funds were in short supply and that I would need to supplement earnings in other ways.

Since I had previously performed with a high school dance band

and later with vocal groups, I decided to put together a dance band to play wedding receptions and other special events. In those days, musicians were well paid, and it was not unusual for each band member to make half a week's wages or more in just one evening. With a bit of advertising, calls came in, and we scheduled our band for mostly Friday and Saturday evening events.

Our band opened for the brand-new Bellaire bowling alley and to a packed house each night. Weekend gigs provided badly needed funds for the individual band members.

A highlight of our existence as a dance band came about on a New Year's Eve in the late 1970s, when we were asked to play for a large community dance in a private school gym. Except for fifteen-minute breaks on the hour, we played for six hours straight, from nine o'clock New Year's Eve until three a.m. the following morning. We did not have six hours of continuous music in the band's repertoire, so we needed to begin repeating numbers we had performed early in the evening. By that time, dancers didn't know the difference or simply didn't care. At the end, the organizers presented us with a check amounting to seventy-five dollars each. At that time, many people worked all week for that amount of money. But, providing six continuous hours of music, singing and playing into microphones, exhausted us to the bone. Dead tired, we walked off the bandstand and sat around a table, talking wearily and trying to recoup. All the equipment had yet to be packed and brought to our vehicles. Then there would be the long drive home where we would expect to arrive at about five a.m.

As I sat with the other musicians around the table, I came to a decision. We had been playing weekend gigs for nearly two years. The six-hour event had brought me to the end of the rope. I announced to the band that they were free to go on without me, but that I had played my last note, at least for the foreseeable future. Overcome by total fatigue, none of them seemed interested in future gigs, and at that point, our band was essentially folded.

It wasn't long, however, until the urge to be involved in music came back into the picture. On two occasions, I performed in the tenor section of the Bellaire Community Choir. I was intrigued, however, by the beat and jazzy sound of southern gospel music.

The first attempt to form a male southern gospel group did not succeed, as group members seemed unable to get into the feel and rhythm of the southern gospel style. Soon thereafter, a mixed quartet was formed which was comprised of two women and two men. A

The Messengers of Melody l to r: Reg, Jamie Cram, Nancy Maurer, Jerry Klooster and Loretta Jacobs on piano.

former Dixieland jazz piano player was added to the group. We were known as The Messengers of Melody.

After one year, our lead singer moved away, and she was replaced by a young lady from a nearby town. At that point, the group was made up of Jamie Cram from Kalkaska on the lead part, Nancy Maurer from Bellaire was on alto, Jerry Klooster from Ellsworth held down the bass part, and Loretta Jacobs was on piano. I covered the tenor part and scheduled the gigs.

We were busy. One year we performed as many as fifty concerts in churches, school gyms, and concert halls. We recorded two studio albums. Highlights of our years of traveling were our two concerts in Hockstad Auditorium in Traverse City where we fronted both the Kingsmen Quartet from Asheville, North Carolina, and the Speer Family from Nashville, Tennessee.

The Messengers of Melody was on the road for a substantial period of time, but relocation of a group member, retirement of our piano player, and other interests of group members eventually led to disbandment of the gospel quartet.

At about this same time, I learned about a newly formed concert band in the nearby town of East Jordan. Throughout my high school years, band practice had been one of the highlights of my day. This was the first time I had known of an adult concert band within geographical range, and I decided to give it a try. There was a problem, however.

An accident during my time in the army had resulted in damage to the ulnar nerve in my right arm. This made it difficult for me to cover all of the valves of a clarinet. I had always enjoyed the sound of a trombone, however, and there were no valves to cover. I drove to Gaylord and went to the Marshall Music Store. There, I found a used trombone for sale at a price of two hundred dollars. I bought it. Now, however, I needed to learn how to play it.

Fortunately, I was able to arrange for trombone lessons from the band teacher at a nearby school district. After five lessons, I took my trombone to a practice session of the Jordan Valley Community Band and sat in with the trombone section.

Being confronted with totally unfamiliar trombone music in a band setting was challenging, to say the least. I was unable to play nearly all of the music in my trombone folder. Nevertheless, I soldiered on, and by the time of the December Christmas Concert, I was able to play enough second trombone music to avoid embarrassment. The Jordan Valley Community Band continues to play, and I remain a member to this day.

As part of the Jordan Valley Community Band, my trombone comes to life in the annual Christmas concert.

My undergraduate degree included a major in physical education. In a teacher training institution such as my alma mater, Western Michigan University, rhythmic movement is normally an integral part of the curriculum. Consequently, ballroom dancing seemed to fall into place for me. As adults, Marilyn and I took dance lessons and attended social dances when the opportunity was offered. When we participated at these dances, however, we recognized something was missing.

My experience as a ballroom dancer, as well as musician, confirmed to me that the majority of bandleaders do not recognize the particular dance style affiliated with the music they are playing. As a result, dancers might be presented, for example, with three swing dances in a row. The continued exertion can exhaust older folks and result in disappointment among dancers. My sound system sat idle in a storage room. A dance band with a properly arranged set list could fill a need.

Musicians were contacted. Gigs were played at Bellaire for the benefit of Friends of Veterans and at the Barnard Grange. Then, COVID-19 hit, and bands such as our Brighter Day Band was totally without gigs.

Recently, we were temporarily able to play gigs again. But, then, a second wave of the COVID virus invaded the population, and the sound system is, again, back in the storage room.

In the meantime, son-in-law Bill Bock fulfilled a longtime desire. As an adult, he learned to play the guitar, proving again that it's never too late. From time to time, Bill and I have been able to get together for a bit of jamming.

I'm not sure how it happened, but somehow I had become editor of my high school newspaper. Perhaps I brought it up at a student council meeting, and I became editor by default. From early on, I had been a top-notch speller and reader. Those skills likely transferred over to my ability to write. Instead of studying for classes, where I was usually poorly prepared, I was apt to be in the business education room, pounding out stories and gossip on a school typewriter.

Upon entering Western Michigan College, I was assigned to a freshman writing (rhetoric) class taught by a Mrs. Burge. PhDs were rare at that time, and Mrs. Burge likely was in possession of a master's degree. She was a quiet, matronly woman. But, I soon found out there was another side to Mrs. Burge.

A theme needed to be written every week and on a topic she designated. Gathering all my journalistic skills, I submitted my first creative writing piece with expectation of a very high grade, perhaps along with a note commending me on my outstanding writing ability. I eagerly anticipated the return of my graded theme. Alas! When my graded paper was returned, it was obvious that Mrs. Burge and I were not on the same page.

A big, red C- topped the cover. I wondered, "Could there be some mistake?"

No. Red corrective marks were all through my paperwork. It was obvious that I had considerable work ahead of me.

Gradually, by following the direction of Mrs. Burge, my grades began to improve. B grades became common. I signed up for Mrs. Burge's class for the second semester. My last theme of the year received a grade of A- along with the words of commendation that I so eagerly sought.

Mrs. Burge was a quiet, gracious woman but a demanding teacher. There are those who write much better than I do. But, because of Mrs. Burge, I became a much better writer. Later, after our family arrived in Bellaire, I was able to earn badly needed income with those writing skills.

As our expenses increased and our income slowed, freelance magazine and newspaper pieces began to make their way from my manual typewriter. It didn't earn enough for a livelihood, but it was a welcome supplement to our diminished income. One magazine article resulted from a trip Marilyn and I had taken to Three Rivers Stadium, at that time the home of the Pittsburgh Pirates, and from an interview with a local prominent athlete.

Roger Mason, a retired Major League Baseball pitcher, resides in our local community. Roger is a devout Christian, and he very graciously gave his approval to submit a story about him to the *Fellowship of Christian Athletes* magazine.

COURAGE ON THE MOUND
ROGER MASON TRAVELS THE LONG ROAD BACK TO THE BIG LEAGUES
By Reg Sprik

It was an August night in 1991 and the Pittsburgh Pirates were clinging to a narrow four-game lead in the National League East pennant race. The Pirates were battling the St. Louis Cardinals and held a one-run advantage midway in the game. But St. Louis had the bases loaded with nobody out.

Quickly, Pirates manager Jim Leyland called timeout and hurried to the pitcher's mound. Right arm raised, he signaled down to the Pittsburgh bullpen.

Suddenly, through the bullpen gate and onto the field strode a tall, strong, but unfamiliar figure. The crowd was puzzled, and for good reason. Except for an obscure inning with the Houston Astros and a couple of pitches at New York's Shea Stadium, it had been four years since Roger Mason had walked onto a major league field.

A former starting pitcher for the Detroit Tigers and San Francisco Giants, Roger Mason had traveled a long and courageous road back to the big leagues. The fact that Roger arrived in professional baseball at all is contrary to all logic.

The second of seven children in a Christian, working-class family, Roger was brought up in Bellaire, Mich., a small northern town where very little baseball is played beyond high school. From his earliest years, however, Roger had his heart set on becoming a pro baseball player.

But in spite of his outstanding high school pitching record, his college pitching achievements and several tryout camps, Roger received no pro offers. Yet, the spark of hope deep within Roger Mason never died out. He decided to give it one more try.

Putting forth his best efforts, Roger received no encouragement from the scouting staff in charge of the camp. Returning home, he decided to put baseball behind him and go on with his life. But totally unexpected, a letter from the Detroit Tigers arrived in Roger's mailbox. In it was an invitation to spring training and a minor league contract.

Four years later, after working up through the Detroit farm system, Roger stood on the Tiger Stadium mound. "It was as if I were living out a dream," Roger remarked. But the dream was short lived.

Traded to San Francisco and moved into the starting rotation, Roger's baseball career was nearly struck down by painful and debilitating tendonitis of the pitching elbow. Surgery and rehabilitation followed, but the arm did not respond. "Some mornings I couldn't even straighten my arm, much less pitch," Roger explained.

Roger unexpectedly was introduced to Dr. Robert Harris, an Australian chiropractic physician temporarily residing near the Mason apartment. "I believe I can relieve your elbow pain," he offered. Two weeks later, after a series of treatments, the pain and stiffness were gone, never to return.

"There is no doubt that God brought our paths together," Roger stated. "Things don't just happen accidently that way."

Traded to Houston, assigned to the minors and eventually released, Roger found himself walking the streets of his hometown as the 1990 baseball season began. But the Pittsburgh Pirates saw potential in Roger. He was signed and sent to Buffalo where he soon began to turn in one splendid mound performance after another. When a Pirate reliever became disabled, Roger was called up.

Roger Mason in his Major League Uniform.

So, on that August night last year, Roger Mason calmly toed the rubber. His relaxed, confident bearing seemed almost out of place for someone just up from the minors. Quickly, the side was retired without a run being scored.

"I knew I had been able to get people out in the past," Roger said. "Besides, I can relax out there because God's only requirement of me is to do my best. I leave the outcome in His hands."

It's a perspective that has continued to work for Roger, as he finished out the season with three appearances in the National League Championship Series, throwing four and a third innings of relief without allowing a single run.

As important as his baseball career is to him, Roger says his family and his Christian witness are his top priorities. As one of a group of Christian baseball players, Roger had an opportunity to visit the Soviet Union shortly before its breakup. Roger and the other players passed out Bibles and gave their testimonies. "The Russian people are hungry for the Word," Roger stated. "We ran out of Bibles."

At home, Roger has assumed a leadership role in an effort to revise the local school system's sex education program. "We emphasize 'sex respect' wherein students learn that abstinence is the only right, sensible, and safe approach to boy-girl relationships."

Roger and his wife, Terry, each teaches a Sunday School class in their home church where they and their two children worship regularly. Roger expressed his concern regarding young adults, commenting that, "so many of them stop attending church beyond middle school and high school age."

Roger credits God for guiding him through the trying times of his baseball career. "My parents saw to it that I was in church and Sunday School. But 10 years ago, while reading a book on prophecy, I realized I had to come to terms with the Lord on a personal basis. At that time, I accepted Jesus Christ as Lord of my life."

"I am not a ballplayer who happens to be a Christian. I am a Christian who happens to be a ballplayer. My ability is God given and is used for God's glory, not for the glory of Roger Mason. That's the whole reason I'm in this – for God to be glorified."

"Whether we are wood carvers or ballplayers, we are to be stewards of our talents as well as stewards of our money. I'm not the story. God is the story."

Reg Sprik is a free-lance writer in Bellaire, Mich.

As an avid reader, I had been intrigued with the idea of spending time on a tropical island. Such a vacation seemed out of financial reach, however, until we heard about a campground on just such an island.

We had retired a few years earlier, and we were thinking about a break from the cold Michigan winter. Through a reliable source, we learned that we could tent camp at Cinnamon Bay Campground in the US Virgin Islands for about thirty dollars per night. The campground was in a national park on St. John Island. By taking midweek flights and by packing our tent and camping gear, we reasoned that this particular island vacation would be economically doable. We bought plane tickets and made campground reservations.

For two weeks, we lived a scene from a tropical movie. Throughout the daylight and evening hours, shorts and T-shirts served as our only necessary apparel. Coconut palm trees provided shade.

Parts of each day were spent lounging on the white sand beach, and we went to sleep listening to the surf rolling in and out on the nearby shore. We usually took advantage of the campground cafeteria for meals three times each day. In the evening, we listened to live steelpan musicians playing music of the islands. A grocery store was located in the nearby town of Cruz Bay, for the few groceries we needed.

From time to time, we took an open-air taxi to and from Cruz Bay for an evening meal and to look through the various stores and gift shops. Buildings were without walls, and a bantam rooster strolled around a restaurant where we enjoyed an evening meal. A couple years later, we repeated our adventure on St. John Island.

Shortly after moving into our new Bellaire home, we learned about a nearby outback trail that had recently been developed. A primitive campground provided an overnight respite for those wishing to make the two-day trek. The trailhead was only a thirty-minute drive from our house. Although we were experienced campers, we had never hiked a trail. Not surprisingly, we were poorly equipped for the Jordan River Pathway.

Marilyn was carrying a suitable pack, but I had borrowed a somewhat dilapidated Boy Scout pack. We did not encounter anyone throughout our entire hike, and the midpoint campground was completely vacant. On the return to our vehicle, the temperature rose substantially, and we began to struggle against the intense heat.

With my poorly fitting backpack taking its toll on my body, I dumped water from my canteen to reduce weight. As we labored up the final hill, our vehicle was a welcome sight.

Closing the door on our teaching careers, Marilyn and I had an opportunity to fulfill some of our travel plans. On one occasion, we took our two oldest grandchildren with us to Toronto, Ontario. Jason (Sprik) and Rob (Bock) were particularly impressed with Canada's Wonderland, where they rode a skyscraping roller coaster. It was their first such experience.

The long, cold winter following our retirement nudged us from our Bellaire home. The resulting journey can best be described by the following letter we sent to family members after our return:

Marilyn and brother Don join me for some Florida sunshine as we visit shortly after retiring from our teaching positions.

This trip probably would not have taken place if it had not been for the annual invitation from brother Don and his wife, Edna, to visit them at their place in Lady Lake, Florida. Now retired, we had no good reason not to go, particularly when Don and Edna practically sold the wheels out from under themselves in order to get us there. But the used conversion van we had bought from them ran beautifully all the way there and back without a single breakdown, and the vehicle contributed greatly to our enjoyment of this little tour. The weather was ideal throughout our venture, except for one day when it rained for a while before the sun broke through.

After picking up Margaret Carlson, Marilyn's mother, we had wheeled out of town at about 6:30 a.m. Wednesday, March 7—not too well rested. Work, scheduled to be done on the van earlier in the week, had been unavoidably delayed, and a guy by the name of Wally and I worked well into Tuesday night finishing the job.

We dropped off Marilyn's mother at the home of her good friend, Skip, who lived alone in her luxurious home on the outskirts of Kalamazoo, then headed down U.S. 131. Shortly after passing over the Indiana state line, we were slowed down by—guess what—a horse and buggy. We were nearing the second largest Amish community in America, centered around Shipshewana, Indiana. Horses and buggies were everywhere. Women were in black, full-length dresses and black bonnets. Slender, bearded men wore black pants and suitcoats, stiff collars, with black shoes and wide-brimmed black hats. I approached one Amish man to ask a question. He was a bit apprehensive but friendly.

"Where can we find a place that serves Amish food?" I asked.

"Try the restaurant over at the sale barn."

I visualized eating a hamburger surrounded by bawling calves and squealing hogs with fragrance to match. Actually, it was nothing of the kind. It was in a clean, separate building, with cauliflower soup that called for a second bowl.

When we finished eating, we went to the "junk" auction barn. What a scene!! If you can see it, feel it, or smell it, someone will buy it. Three animal bones together with a single spindly deer antler sold for three dollars.

From Shipshewana, we traveled down through Indiana and into Kentucky's hilly southwest region before calling it a day. We had done alright for day one and we were near the entrance to one of the seven Natural Wonders of the World—Mammoth Cave. We discovered an excellent campground outside the cave entrance.

On Thursday, we took two tours into the cave. One was a descent to the part of the cave containing stalactites (down-hangers, like icicles) and stalagmites (up-standers, like large posts). It was fascinating. We also took the historical tour which went down through the old mines of Civil War days, still in mint condition. We learned that wood timbers do not deteriorate in caves. At one point, we were three hundred feet beneath the surface when the guide turned out all the lights. Total darkness. The guide calmed everybody down by telling all group members to stay together because in the past some people had become lost in the cave.

"I can understand how that can happen," he reassured everyone, "because I've been lost down here a few times myself."

We stayed at a campground near Nashville that night and left on Route 65 the next morning. There was way too much semitruck traffic. Instead, we traveled on two-lane back country roads into Alabama. There we had a chance to leisurely look around at the way the people of the area live. Eastern Alabama and western Georgia is timber country with a little other agriculture thrown in. Here and there, we saw evidence of industry's flight from the state of Michigan. Manufacturing names, familiar to us in Michigan, were located down there in brand new buildings, in towns that looked as if they were remnants of the Civil War. The new plants looked strange there and out of place.

Cruising through southern Georgia, we saw almost no out-of-state license plates. We were off the beaten path on two-lane roads (well maintained, however). People in cars and on the roadside waved to us like old neighbors. Traffic was local and light. One day we saw only one other RV that appeared to be traveling through.

Poor folk live in southern Georgia. It is another world, or at least like another country. Segregation exists, not by law but by heritage and environment. Economically too, it is a subsistence living. The kids grow up in it. How can a young person rise above it if that person has never seen anything other than what he or she lives in? It is the standard for them. They know nothing else.

It was overnight in Georgia and on down to Lady Lake, Florida, on Saturday. Don and Edna were glad to see us, and we likewise. We stayed there through Thursday night. During that time, we took in Disney World with old friend Phil Batts and his wife, Loraine, a couple of great guides. Phil and Loraine live in Florida near Disney World and have been there many times. They knew just how to get around, and we saw nearly everything there was to see in the Magic Kingdom.

The next day, Don and Edna invited us to join them in a best ball golf tournament at Blue Parrot Campground where they live. Strange as it may seem, we did not win. The day before that, though, Don had shot a score of twenty-eight for nine holes—a personal record for him. Although the course is shorter than normal with a lot of par threes, that was a pretty good bit of golf.

Backing up a bit, we need to tell you we surprised some of our friends, Chuck and Connie, by showing up unannounced at one of their Florida concerts. They were shocked, to say the least, and as glad to see us as we were to see them. They had been on concert tour in the south since January and would not return home to Bellaire, Michigan, until May.

On Wednesday, Don and Edna took us to the Kennedy Space Center for a most interesting day. This is a must if you spend any time around central Florida. A person cannot really get a true picture of the spacecraft by watching television. It boggled the mind to see the unbelievable size of these spacecraft and components, as well as the almost super-human technology involved. It was truly amazing what the mind of man had achieved in such a relatively short period of time.

Thursday morning it was on to SeaWorld where we saw leaping dolphins, women and men riding the backs of killer whales, a water ski extravaganza, and on and on. Different shows keep a person going all day long. It is expensive, like about everything else, but well worth the money. We enjoyed it immensely.

Also, while we were there at the campground, Don and I did special music for a hymn sing. We didn't have much time to practice, but some people told us they enjoyed our music.

On Friday morning at 4:30, we were on our way to Georgia—this time on a different route. Moving through Georgia, we headed into South Carolina, and before 7 p.m., we were in Reynolds Auditorium in Winston-Salem, North Carolina, ready to take in a concert by the Speers and the Florida Boys. The concert was just great. We had covered more than seven hundred miles that day.

Saturday was a rather relaxing day as we waited to take in the Hallelujah Supper Club at Newton, North Carolina, for dinner and a concert following. We had made reservations earlier. The Vanguards were on stage that night. They were very good, although not quite in the same league with the Speers or the Kingsmen Quartet.

On Sunday morning, we began to notice a bit of a chill in the air. We pointed the van into the Blue Ridge Mountains again where we had gone earlier on Saturday, when we went up to the mountain town of Blowing Rock. Again, the beautiful scenery continued in the mountains through Virginia. We moved on through West Virginia's old coal mining towns and on into Ohio. There, in Ohio, we stopped to see and hear the Fishermen Quartet; they were in concert in a Methodist church in the small farming community of Nevada (rhymes with putata, you know, like with gravy).

Since we had traveled so far to be at their concert, the Fishermen dedicated a song to us. It was a packed house, and we thoroughly enjoyed the Fishermen. Monday it was back to Kalamazoo to pick up Marilyn's mother, and on home where it is always Home Sweet Home.

While we were gone, we traveled mostly side roads, away from tourist signs and promotional glitz. We were in and through eleven states and saw a wide variety of lands and waters. We met many very nice people who always said, "Y'all come back," and we saw old friends including Mary Alice Burke Garn, who graduated with me from Manton High School and her husband, Maynard, who also went to school with me at Manton. We spent an enjoyable evening reminiscing. We also had a chance to visit one afternoon with my cousin, Chester Sprik, who lives near Lady Lake, and who we hadn't seen for thirty-five years.

Following is a travel article published in the Traverse City Record Eagle describing a whitewater rafting adventure Marilyn and I experienced in West Virginia.

Trip to a Whitewater Rafting Adventure (Special to the Record-Eagle)
Traverse City Record-Eagle Sunday, November 8, 1992
By REG SPRIK

FAYETTEVILLE, W.V. – Our river guide was having trouble being heard above the mounting roar of the Class V rapids ahead.

"Everybody paddle! Go hard!" he yelled.

Seemingly out of control, our eight-person raft turned sideways and plunged down into a threatening, steep-sided water trough. Spray was erupting all around us and we were getting drenched. We looked ahead. The water was above our heads. Panicky screams could barely be heard above the thundering water.

Pausing for a split second, as if to gather strength, the raft suddenly surged forward, up and over the rising plume of water, barely missing a room-sized boulder on its way down.

Bouncing along over somewhat milder rapids below, we looked around and found all our paddlers still on board. Rafters in other boats were not so lucky. Two people were catapulted overboard, but were quickly pulled to safety. No one was injured. We had just passed through another stretch of whitewater on the lower New River at the bottom of West Virginia's 1,000-foot-deep New River Gorge.

From the time I began reading about adventure travel, I had been intrigued by the idea of whitewater rafting. My wife was not quite so enthusiastic.

"Go right ahead," Marilyn said. "I'll wait for you in the car. No way will I climb into one of those rafts!"

But as the time approached, she began having second thoughts. And finally agreed to go.

"I may not come back alive," I overheard her tell our daughter over the telephone.

We had written to the West Virginia Division of Tourism and Parks at Charleston and got a colorful, comprehensive booklet loaded with information and advertising about whitewater rafting, including 800 numbers for the rafting companies.

We called several outfitters and looked over the brochures each sent in reply. We finally settled on a booking with Passages to Adventure, located at Fayetteville.

When we arrived at Passages' headquarters, we registered and signed waivers absolving the outfitter from liability in case of injury or death. (Some say these waivers are worthless in a court of law.) About 60 rafters were milling around in the souvenir shop, buying various items and waiting to get started.

We were provided with special rafting helmets, and Type 1 life jackets, the kind that roll a wearer over and keep his or her face above water even if the victim in unconscious. Then we climbed aboard Passages' converted school buses and headed down the switchbacks to our take-off point.

When the rafts were unloaded we were assigned to a guide, who reviewed safety policies and procedures. We pushed our raft off into a quiet pool where we spent several minutes practicing paddling techniques and responses to the river guide's specific directions.

It was reassuring to note that these rafts were sturdy contraptions, to say the least. They were not made of rubber, a material that could easily rip open on a sharp rock, but instead, were constructed of a heavy, rugged type of canvas, permeated, and heavily coated with a high-grade plastic material. Each raft costs about $3,500.

A highlight of our adventure was the delicious and ample shore lunch provided by Passages. No stale, crusty sandwiches and cold coffee here. Using the inverted rafts for tables, we were treated to sliced ham, turkey and beef with Swiss and American cheese, on whole wheat or white bread. There was potato salad, macaroni salad, carrot sticks and a dip.

Dessert was chocolate pudding and chocolate chip cookies. All with plenty of ice-cold Kool-aid to wash it all down.

Then it was on to the river and the rapids.

At the end of our river journey, we were bused back to Passages' headquarters where, at a reasonable price, we were offered photos of us taken on our way through whitewater. A guide had positioned himself on a boulder directly below one of the rapids and had taken several shots of each raft hurtling through the whitewater.

And the price? We thought it was the adventure bargain of the decade, perhaps of a lifetime. The total cost for Marilyn and me was less than $100, including 6 percent West Virginia sales tax. Other outfitter's fees are in the same general price range – between $45 and $65 per day, per person.

A lot depends on the day of the week one runs the river. Mid-week prices are usually lower, and some outfitters give a discount to senior citizens and AAA members. Don't hesitate to ask about special discounts.

Several campgrounds and motels are available in the area. A good place to get information is the Canyon Rim Visitor Center, located directly north of the New River Gorge Bridge on U.S. 19 near Fayetteville.

Is this for everyone? Well, almost. Anyone over 12 years of age and in reasonably good health should not hesitate. It is a unique adventure that will remain in one's memory for a lifetime.

Whitewater rafting: We careen wildly through the New River whitewater, paddling desperately for raft control.

In spite of her apprehensions, Marilyn became a convert. On the way home she said she'd be up for another try some day.

Passages to Adventure schedule whitewater trips from March to October, but river conditions vary considerably during that span. It's best to get specific details in advance.

- Chapter Eleven -
Loss and Reflection

Four days after our fifty-sixth wedding anniversary, I lost my beautiful wife, Marilyn. It was an indescribable loss. It was like the tearing away of a part of me. I was totally devastated.

Marilyn taught elementary school children for eighteen
years after our children were in school.

Without a doubt, others before me were correct when they told their stories about the length of time that had elapsed before they were able to right their emotional ship after such a terrible loss. It has now been nearly fifteen years since that awful day. I had been warned not to make major decisions in the aftermath of losing my lovely marriage partner, and I have not made any that could not be undone.

I never want to forget the good times Marilyn and I had together, and I still shed a tear when I look at her photo on the living room piano. That will probably never change, nor do I want it to change. But, I have a wonderful family that has stood by my side through my ordeal, and, although I still miss Marilyn terribly, my grief is no longer all-consuming. Music, support of my family, and good friends have helped me along the way.

As is undoubtedly the case with most of us who have been married for a significant period of time, there is an ongoing sharing of nearly every aspect of life. Nearly every decision is a shared one: finances, social plans, travel, and on and on. Even my solo fishing ventures out on the local streams and lakes were shared experiences.

"Oh, those are nice ones! We can have those for supper," she would say, as she admired my catch of the day.

But now, the former enjoyment found in my fishing excursions is no longer there.

Marilyn never asked me when I was coming home whenever I left with my rod and reel or shotgun in hand. When I came home, she would often have fed the family and put my supper in the fridge. She never complained about the time I spent in the field or on the trout stream. For just that simple, unselfish attitude, among her other qualities, I will forever be grateful to her.

Likewise, when Marilyn went shopping in Traverse City, I never asked her when she was coming home. All of this reflected the love and respect we had for each other.

As my time with Marilyn came to an end, I thought about the significance of our fiftieth wedding anniversary celebration.

Daughters Jan and Nancy had arranged for the rental of a hall in Petoskey. They decorated it beautifully. Our two daughters managed the food situation, and the Gary Stutzman Band provided dance music. It was a wonderful and memorable occasion, a highlight of our fifty-six-year marriage.

Below is a talk I prepared for friends and relatives at Marilyn's memorial. I did not read this. I used it as a reference, however.

"Thank you" to all of you from the bottom of my heart for coming here today to pay tribute to Marilyn and to support our family. I know I speak for all of our extended family, as well.

And, I want to personally thank my kids, grandkids, and their marriage partners for standing by my side through this terribly difficult time.

The question is often asked, "How did you two meet?"

Well, we met at a college dance while we were students at Western Michigan University. We met in the fall of 1950 and were married the following August 24. To tell the truth, I never understood what she saw in me. My hunting and fishing friends are quick to agree. They can't figure it out, either.

Some very special experiences we shared were: Haying time on the farm we lived on for nine years, camping trips with our kids through the west, and visiting national parks, camping with family in the Canadian Outback. Also, going to ball fields, football stadiums, gyms, and tracks to watch our kids participate. Plus, attending southern gospel music concerts and vacations in Toronto. It goes on. What a journey it was. But, far and away, Marilyn's biggest interest was her family.

She loved music and hated the water unless the pool was well heated. Basically a private person, Marilyn loved to read, she loved her home, and she loved flowers.

Marilyn always thought of others and rarely thought about herself. She didn't have it in her to say a bad word about anybody. And if she were standing next to me now, she would almost certainly say, "Oh, come on. Let's talk about something else."

This is Marilyn's obituary, which I wrote shortly after her passing:

Marilyn Sprik
Died August 28, 2007

BELLAIRE – Marilyn Sprik, of Bellaire, passed away peacefully Tuesday, Aug. 28, 2007, after a 10-year determined and courageous battle with a rare neurological condition. Although nearly completely paralyzed, she remained aware of her surroundings until the very end.

Born in Detroit on Jan. 13, 1932, she was adopted shortly after birth by Roy and Margaret Carlson. She was their only child.

Marilyn was a graduate of Kalamazoo State High School, where her sunny disposition brought her many lasting friends. She then attended Western Michigan University for one year before marrying Reg Sprik on August 24, 1951, in Kalamazoo.

When her children were well along in school, Marilyn resumed her education, earning a bachelor of arts degree and elementary teacher certification from Western Michigan University.

She then taught elementary children for 18 years before retiring at 57. During her early teaching days, she taught for two years at a one-room country school comprised of grades K through 8.

A few years prior to her retirement, along with her husband, she began running three-mile and longer road races. A highlight of her athletic achievements was running the eight-mile road race around Mackinac Island.

Some of her most enjoyable times took place during the nine years she, Reg, and the children lived on their 41-acre farm with horses and assorted farm animals.

Marilyn was a private person who loved to read. She also greatly enjoyed watching her children participate in school and college athletics and cheerleading.

Marilyn particularly enjoyed attending church services with her family, southern gospel music concerts, and big musicals on both stage and screen. She also loved to camp, and along with her family, enjoyed two memorable camping excursions through the Dakotas, Wyoming, and Montana. Later, she and her husband tent camped two different times in the U.S. Virgin Islands. She was dedicated to land conservation.

Marilyn is survived by Reg, her husband of 56 years. Also surviving are her children, David (Cheryl) Sprik of Central Lake and Orlando Fla., Robert (Robin) Sprik of Lowell, Jan (Bill) Bock of Bellaire and Nancy

(Jim) Vanden Broek of Bellaire. Also surviving are 11 grandchildren and seven great-grandchildren.

She was predeceased by her parents and two grandchildren.

Marilyn's final resting place is in the Arlene (Caldwell Township) Cemetery, located between Manton and Lake City, where she and Reg have reserved space in the Sprik family plot.

No services are planned, but a celebration of Marilyn's life will be announced at a later date.

Should you wish to pay tribute to Marilyn's memory, please donate to the Cadillac Area Land Conservancy, 3860 North Long Lake Road, Suite D, Traverse City, MI 49684-9601.

Marilyn – Mom – Grandma, We love you. We love you beyond words.

Please share thoughts and memories with the family on their online guest book at www.legacy.com/record-eagle/.

Arrangements are by Young Funeral Home of Lake City.

I know of no event comparable to the unexpected loss of a young family member. I had witnessed it earlier in life when my eighteen-year-old brother, Ray, lost his life after his appendix ruptured and peritonitis set in.

My dad, a quiet man, would sometimes ask me to go for a ride with him in his dump truck, our only means of transportation at that time. Driving over dusty roads to a country cemetery, he would kneel down in front of my brother's headstone, remove his hat, and pour out his soul in audible prayer. Those scenes, depicting my dad's inconsolable grief, were burned into my memory.

About a year after Marilyn had passed away, "Dad, Dad, wake up."

The dim night light showed the outline of my daughter Nancy and her husband, Jim. The clock read 4 a.m. I immediately realized something terrible had happened. It was worse than I could have imagined.

"It's Lisa," Nancy said. "She was killed in a car wreck."

At first, I had trouble coming to terms with the total situation. Lisa was a twenty-one-year-old senior at Lake Superior State University. I thought about my daughter Jan and her husband, Bill. How would they endure this traumatic sudden loss of their only daughter? I felt a sense of helplessness.

Our family is very close-knit, and we all did everything we could to provide support. Still, after others resume daily lives, a cloud of seemingly unending grief continues to hang over the immediate family. Lisa was such a bright, shining light.

Lisa will always live on in our memories.

As land development had started to become an issue in northwestern Lower Michigan, Marilyn and I had become increasingly concerned as to the future of our fifty-two-acre property in the Arlene community in Missaukee County. Forty acres of this property had been in the Sprik family since 1917. After Marilyn and I had left the scene, would subsequent owners possibly subdivide the property and spoil its natural beauty?

Marilyn and I had put the property under the protection of the Cadillac Area Land Conservancy and gifted shares of the property to our four children. Marilyn and I retained equal shares.

Soon after Marilyn's passing, and without my knowledge, the family built a cabin on the Arlene property. Son-in-law Bill Bock engineered the project. Grandsons Andy Bock and Kyle Aldrich worked with Bill, Dave and son-in-law Jim Vanden Broek to complete the project. Bill made sure the building was rodent proof. Over the years, this has served as a hunting cabin and a retreat for various family members.

Building the cabin retreat at the Arlene property.

Looking across the landscape from the finished cabin deck.

The home that Marilyn and I built sits atop a hill. The one-eighth-mile driveway provides an excellent sledding hill in the cold Michigan winter. Once a year, usually in February, a bonfire is built, and a Saturday afternoon becomes somewhat of a sledding circus. Hot cocoa, hot dogs, and marshmallows offer nourishment. All family and extended family members are invited.

Grandson Kyle Aldrich shares an afternoon of sledding down our Bellaire home driveway.

Living alone and with time on my hands, my urge to travel gradually came back into the picture. Over time, I visited the Sleeping Bear Dunes National Lakeshore, relatives in Florida, the national parks of Utah, and a friend in California.

Nancy shares a trip to the land of our ancestors, as we navigate through Amsterdam and the Netherlands countryside.

I flew twice to the Netherlands, once accompanied by daughter Nancy and, along with relatives and friends, attended several Western Michigan University football games. But, soon after Marilyn's memorial, the memory of our days on the St. John tropical paradise came flooding back. I wanted to relive those memories, so I packed my tent and headed out. Strolling a street in the town of Cruz Bay, I saw a sign on a post advertising a sailboat trip to Jost Van Dyke, an island in the British Virgin Islands. I recognized the name of the sailboat captain, who I had coincidentally met earlier in the week. A telephone call booked me for passage. The captain reminded me to bring my passport.

A honeymooning couple from Minneapolis were the only other passengers. A female mate assisted the captain.

"Whale," yelled the mate, as the Jost Van Dyke Harbor appeared in the distance.

We watched as the whale blew a stream of water high in the air. The captain turned the sailboat in the direction of the whale, in order to get a closer look. Suddenly, a second whale surfaced within the distance of a football field. We surmised that they were a mating pair. "They're humpbacks," the captain explained.

Tying up at the harbor dock, the captain took our passports to the British Consul Office. After lunch at a local café and a brief walking tour, we sailed back to Cruz Bay. By that time the whales had moved out. We did not encounter another boat during our ocean venture, and the quietness and peacefulness of the journey left a lasting impression.

Although I had been stationed near Washington, DC, during my army days at Fort Dix, I had not taken advantage of my opportunity to see the historical sites in our nation's capital. So, I made flight and lodging arrangements through a travel agency and wrote it on my calendar. Meanwhile, daughter Nancy and her husband, Jim, had made plans for a road trip through the Mid-Atlantic states, including a stay in DC to see the sights. We connected at the Holiday Inn Capitol, and after perusing pertinent maps and literature, we wrote down our plans for the next several days.

Our first day of venturing out brought us to the Spy Museum. We learned that spies are likely somewhere among us. They are people of all walks of life, but they are working undercover for our national government. Their clandestine life of spying is, necessarily, unknown to their wives or husbands and families. In some cases, these individuals go to their grave with their secret lives known only to key people in the FBI or CIA. In many cases, their identity is never disclosed. In other cases, where identities had been brought to light, complete profiles were on display.

Next on our list was Ford's Theatre, where President Abraham Lincoln had been assassinated. Everything in the theatre was just like it was the day Lincoln was shot. This was, indeed, a trip back in time, as with a bit of imagination, one could visualize the president and his wife sitting right there in the presidential box seats.

Although we did not have time to tour the interiors of the White House, Capitol, and other monuments, we were able to get up close enough to get a picture in our minds of what these places are really like.

The National Air and Space Museum, with the history of air travel from its very beginning, was impressive, to say the least. There, we saw the actual space capsules used by Alan Shepard right on through to the moon landers and beyond. Witnessing the claustrophobic

Son-in-law Jim Vanden Broek shares a time of relaxation during Washington, DC, trip.

conditions astronauts endured, I was amazed when I considered the extraordinary courage required by these people who put their lives on the line as they traveled into the unknown. And, as is well known, numerous lives were lost during these endeavors.

I was stunned when I saw the colossal size of the Wright Brothers first airplane. I had no idea it was such a massive flying machine. In retrospect, however, the engineering capabilities of the Wright Brothers were evident when considering the air-lift needed to counteract the weight of the engine, plus that of the pilot, perhaps no less than five hundred pounds.

My flight home was scheduled one day after Jim and Nancy needed to leave Washington, DC. I have always been fascinated by zoological parks, and I decided to spend my final day in the capital at the National Zoo. This is a large and comprehensive facility. The large cats, as well as other large animals, were on display. However, it was the small animal building and its unusual creatures that caught my special attention.

Some of these small animals and birds are in dire need of additional protection to prevent extinction, as happened to our carrier pigeon, which at one time blackened our skies during migration. I was intrigued to learn that some of these small creatures inhabit just a tiny section of one island and can be found in no other locations.

A highly improbable incident took place at the end of my taxi ride back to the airport, however, an occurrence that will undoubtedly never happen to me again. The driver refused to accept my tip, even after I insisted that he take it. There must be a place in heaven for people like this.

I started on three liters of oxygen and gradually escalated to five. I was told I would not be able to go much beyond five liters. I couldn't walk and I was in a wheelchair. Without oxygen I couldn't breathe.

It all started about two years earlier when I gradually became unable to walk more than the length of a football field before stopping to relieve my backache by bending over with hands on knees or sitting. At about the same time I became aware of a decided shortness of breath whenever I walked, danced, or became involved in any activity at up-tempo speed. Over time, the distance I was able to walk before stopping became shorter and shorter. As a long-time distance runner and walker, the idea of being so physically limited caused me to become frustrated and depressed. At the time, I believed my major problem was in my back. A consultation with a neurosurgeon revealed that if I wanted to continue normal walking activities, surgery was my only option. I scheduled a date for the surgery.

Meanwhile, my physical health had declined to some degree, and by the time the surgery date arrived, the surgeon appeared to be somewhat apprehensive as to the wisdom of anesthetizing me. After some hesitation, he decided to proceed with the surgery. The surgery turned out to be more complex than originally thought, and I was under anesthesia for approximately five hours. After three days, I was sent home from the hospital, looking forward to a full recovery. But, alas, my already defective heart valves were unexpectedly traumatized by the back surgery, and after eight days at home, I awoke from an afternoon nap unable to breathe.

In a panic, I grabbed the bedside telephone and dialed 911. During my fifteen-minute wait for the ambulance, I survived by hyperventilating on each breath. Upon arrival, ambulance staff put me on oxygen, and then, inexplicably, the driver drove off in the wrong direction. Fortunately, a plentiful supply of oxygen was aboard the ambulance as the correction was made.

The scene at the Petoskey Hospital was chaotic, as staff dealt with a heavier than normal load of patients. Put simply, there was an inability to determine what was wrong with me, and there was talk of sending me home.

Realizing the nearly certain catastrophic consequences of such a move, I refused to allow that to happen, and I was subsequently moved to a hospital room. Four additional hospitalizations ensued before my primary care physician came to the conclusion that I needed to be transferred to Munson Medical Center in Traverse City if I were to have a chance to survive. At that point, my primary care physician informed my family that I would not live long without corrective surgery. He later told me I might have survived four weeks, at best.

Shortly after my arrival at Munson Medical Center, I was met by Dr. Mack Stirling, the senior member of the four-member thoracic surgery team at Munson. Dr. Stirling explained my surgical plan in a straightforward and gentlemanly way and asked if I had questions. I don't recall having much to say, as I was willing to allow his plan to play out.

At eighty-five years of age, except for my mother who lived to the age of eighty-six, I had outlived everyone in my immediate family.

Prior to my being anesthetized, our church pastor came in to see me, as did three of my children. I assured them that I was okay with whatever might transpire during surgery and not to worry about me. Five hours later, I awoke to the sound of voices.

Although I had not read any of their books, I knew there were others who claimed to have undergone "out-of-body" experiences, during which they observed the people and procedure in the operating room. According to book summaries, at least some of these authors considered themselves to be in a state between life and death. Because I was in my mid-eighties and in declining health, I did not expect to live through the heart surgery. When voices came to my ears, I thought perhaps I might be in some type of surreal existence. But I soon opened my eyes to learn, to my relief, that I was here on planet Earth.

It is impossible to adequately commend people like Drs. Steve Wisniewski and Mack Stirling. They spend every hour of their working lives attempting to save the lives of others.

Dr. Stirling was the head of the thoracic surgery department. I was on the brink of death. My heart surgery was indeed risky, and I believe there was a high possibility that I might not survive. There were several other highly qualified surgeons in his department, but Dr. Stirling took on the surgery himself.

The following letter expresses my gratitude:

March 5, 2017

Dear Dr. Stirling,

Just a note to thank you for giving me another shot. It will soon be four years since I arrived at Munson in a wheelchair and on five liters of oxygen. Dr. Wisniewski told my daughter that I wouldn't last four weeks as is, and he then arranged a transfer to your department. Many thanks to problem solvers.

Just so you know, I'm playing trombone in a concert band as well as playing harmonica and doing vocals in a dance band at the East Jordan Civic Center. In fact, I'm the bandleader.

Since you replaced my valve, I've toured the national parks of Utah and traveled to the Netherlands, the homeland of my ancestors. My mother was an immigrant.

When I'm not playing, I get out to some dances (I'm a decent swing dancer). Along with my running daughter, I get to a few road races. But I only do one-milers instead of 5Ks, and I walk instead of run. When weather permits, I try to get out and hike as often as possible.

I'm living alone in my own home about three miles northeast of Bellaire, and I intend to stay here. They better be careful if they come to get me, as I won't make it easy.

My gratitude is beyond words to you for your surgical skills and willingness to gamble on my toughness, as well as to Steve Wisniewski for "grabbing the bull by the horns" and transferring my care to your department. Life is precious.

Sincerely,

Reg Sprik (Edward R.)

CC: Steve Wisniewski, Memoir Book

My failing heart was not the only issue that could have, and very well might have, affected my health and my overall well-being. Earlier in my life I became acutely aware that the drinking of any beverage containing alcohol impacted me in a way different from the way it affected most people.

Whereas others usually seemed to be satisfied with a drink or two at dinner, or at a social event, the same was not true for me. One drink would, inevitably, trigger an obsession and a craving for more of the same. Often, if I knew only one or two drinks would be available, I would refuse all drinks. It was not surprising, then, that this situation in which I found myself sometimes led to excessive drinking. I decided to seek answers.

I learned that a group of people who shared my problem met weekly in a nearby community. While attending that meeting, I learned that I was one of five percent of the population who shared a common malady. I also learned that the only treatment was total abstinence.

I would much prefer to state that from that day forward, I adhered strictly to the wisdom of those who had gone before. That is not the way my mind works, however. My rebellious nature sometimes took control of my brain, and the results were not good.

It has now been more than forty-seven years since any type of alcoholic drink has crossed my lips, and I have long since lost all desire for alcohol in any form. That compulsion was removed via a sudden spiritual experience similar to that of Bill W., one of the founders of our fellowship.

Fortunately, during those drinking days, I was never ticketed for impaired driving, I was never before a judge, I never lost a job or my family. I was never in any type of rehab. None of those things happened to me. But, any one of them could have happened.

Overall, I don't miss the use of alcohol in any way, and I'm glad to have it out of my life.

It was Thursday evening, January 11, 2018. After straightening out a few items that were a part of my usual household disarray, daughter Nancy informed me that I should be dressed up and prepared to be picked up the following Saturday afternoon, January 13. I didn't know what to expect but I was well aware of a ninetieth birthday, which had just gone by, and I suspected that some sort of event to commemorate that date might have been planned. I had no idea as to its nature.

At the appointed 1 p.m. time, however, Nancy pulled into my rural driveway, and, dressed up to my Sunday best, I joined her for a ride to the unknown somewhere. However, as we rounded the corner heading toward the Bellaire United Methodist Church, I observed a group of vehicles along the road and in the church parking lot. At that point, I realized this was not to be simply a family luncheon.

As Nancy and I proceeded down the steps to the lower level of the church, I was greeted by loud cheers and shouts of "Happy Birthday" by a large gathering of family, extended family, and many very good friends.

Since I am not a local leader or celebrity, I was somewhat taken aback by the large number of folks that continued to stream in. I soon learned that two of my granddaughters, Tiffany Aldrich and Danielle Sprik, were very much involved in arrangements for the occasion, along with my son Dave and daughters Jan and Nancy.

A table of food was provided for everyone throughout the 2:00 p.m. to 5:00 p.m. event. To my considerable surprise, a musician friend, Willie Dahl, was on hand with microphone and sound system to provide music for the occasion.

As might be expected, various friends learned that I was writing an autobiography. "I wish my parents or grandparents had left a record of our family history," they told me. "Now they're gone, and that history is lost."

I encourage everyone to write what you know about your family's past. It doesn't need to be fancy. It can be printed or written in long hand. Better yet, a friend or family member might be willing to type it on a lap-top and run it over to a printer. This book was pounded out on a manual typewriter and then turned over to a person who is adept at laptops.

Nor does it need to be lengthy. I recently read an autobiography written by a local individual who told his story in just over one hundred pages. He took it to the local weekly newspaper office where it was bound in cardboard and plastic. There is another substantial benefit for the writer of an autobiography, however. It can reveal the deep-seated characteristics of the writer.

All my life I had been told that I "didn't measure up" and that "I wasn't good enough." My schoolmates in our country school didn't like me, and several tried to bully me, which proved to be a mistake for the bullies. Each marking period, my mother expressed disappointment in my grades. Our head high school administrator told me, in no uncertain terms, that I was too dumb to go on to college.

During high school days I was falsely accused of setting the wood-shop on fire. The guilty party lied and accused me. Nothing I said could change their minds. All of this did one thing for me—it set me on a journey to prove them wrong.

The same assistant football coach who told me "I wasn't good enough" watched from the sidelines a year later as I ran out on the field during a homecoming game as the starting defensive right tackle. His recruited stars warmed the bench.

Earlier, during high school days, each of us small town boys, on a small school basketball team, combined forces to prove that we were indeed able to "measure up" by winning a State Championship.

With blueprints in our hands and a pile of lumber in the yard, four of us built the house I now live in, and where I've lived for forty-eight years. None of us had ever before built a house.

Throughout my life new ideas regarding activities and adventures continue to enter my brain. Until I sat down to write this book, however, I never realized the full extent of my impulsiveness. For instance, if the tires of my vehicle became wedged between railroad tracks and if a lengthy freight train came roaring down Bunker Hill, car parts might have been distributed throughout Manton and the surrounding countryside. In that case, I would have needed to head for another county, maybe another state, maybe to Australia.

I should have known that Corporal Hamilton was not being truthful when he invited me to accompany him on an errand in an army vehicle. But, hey, life can get boring on an army base and living it up at the roller rink was a rare treat. Now and then, the thought crossed my mind that, "maybe we shouldn't be doing this." Back at the base, word spread quickly and I noticed people looking at me strangely, as if they were thinking, "I wonder if there's something wrong with that guy."

Yet, if it were not for a degree of impulsiveness, and if we had waited for everything to be just right, our spectacular adventures through the mountainous west and national parks would not have taken place.

One of our adventures was with a borrowed tent, a $300.00 loan from a bank, and six of us in a Volkswagen Bug towing a sixteen-foot aluminum boat full of gear and supplies. We had no road service.

From the time our ragtag five-piece band played the school dances at Manton High School, music has been an important part of my life. Looking across the room I see my array of harmonicas. After a long rest due to the pandemic, they will soon be put to use as our dance band is scheduled to play a benefit in the near future.

Furthermore, a concert band is located nearby and I am able to put my trombone to good use.

It is another morning. As I gaze out the wide living room window, I see white, wispy clouds drifting across a beautiful light blue sky. The colors of the sky match the colors of my home. Tall red pines decorate the horizon and there is silence. I am filled with gratitude for the gift of another day.

Acknowledgments

The inspiration for this book occupies a space in front of me on my kitchen table. It is a photo of my beautiful wife, Marilyn. She would have wanted me to write this book.

Many thanks to daughter Jan Bock, who with an assist from daughter, Nancy Vanden Broek, devoted countless hours selectively sorting through envelopes and stacks of photo albums in order to apply suitable photos to the appropriate pages. My gratitude for your dedication to this project is beyond words. This book is yours as much as it is mine.

And to Jack Bodis, owner of *Creative Characters*, thank you for using your vast experience in graphic design, as well as your knowledge of book design and publishing to help get this endeavor into print. Without your help, this book would not be in existence.

If it were not for the high-level computer skills of Paula McKenna, this book would not have seen the light of day. My everlasting "thank you" Paula for taking my scrambled, cobbled-up manuscript and making sense of it. You are a de-scrambling and typing whiz.

A huge thank you to Darlene Short for being willing to gamble on the legibility and organization of a first-time book author. It is my good fortune to have a person of your highly recommended skills as editor and proofreader of my book.

Many of the events described in the final chapters of this book are due to the expert guidance of Doug Watrous. Doug willingly shared his vast knowledge of Bellaire area streams, lakes, and woodlands, and guided members of our family on numerous trips to the Canadian Outback. Thanks, Doug, for your significant contribution to this life story.

A warm note of appreciation to members of the *Messengers*

of Melody Gospel Quartet – Jami, Jerry, Nancy and pianist, Loretta. Your talent and dedication allowed us to record two albums and bring a joyful sound to countless listeners.

A big thank you to band conductor Becky Palmiter, for enduring my off-key trombone notes as I wade through Sousa Marches in the Jordan Valley Community Band. You are blessed with exceptional tolerance.

Playing in a dance band with a floor full of dancers has always been a special experience for me. Much of that enjoyment has to do with the other band members who are all class acts. Thanks for sharing the bandstand with me.

My everlasting gratitude goes out to Dick Lyon, the legendary coach who led our Manton High School Basketball Team to the Class "C" State Championship. We were a team without a star. Dick's calm demeanor kept us focused as we escaped one close call after another on our way to the championship trophy. Our tournament run is described in the preceding pages.

And to Mike Arsnoe, Buz Haltenhoff, Ernie Mindel, Mike Reed and Don Sprik — your timely telephone calls have been a spark moving me forward as I have plodded along through this seemingly endless writing effort. Thanks for the welcome and refreshing words of encouragement.

I owe a deep debt of gratitude to my parents, Ed and Margaret Sprik, who, although struggling mightily through the most difficult of economic times, always saw to it that I was well nourished. In spite of the fact that medical and dental care were practically non-existent, I was always provided with adequate clothing to meet weather conditions. And, although traces of snow, blowing through a faulty window frame, occasionally decorated the top of my bed, I was always supplied with plenty of blankets to ward off the cold.

Many friends and relatives who were an important part of my life are not named in these pages. To all those I extend my deepest apologies. If I were to include everyone who deserves mentioning, the weight of the book would break down my writing table.

Reg Sprik

Made in the USA
Columbia, SC
14 November 2023

26264571R00124